7 Steps to A Super Job

Prem P. Bhalla

GOODWILL PUBLISHING HOUSE®
B-3 Rattan Jyoti, 18 Rajendra Place
New Delhi-110008 (INDIA)

Published by:
GOODWILL PUBLISHING HOUSE
B-3 Rattan Jyoti, 18 Rajendra Place
New Delhi-110008 (INDIA)
Ph.: 25750801, 25820556
Fax: 91-11-25763428
Website: goodwillpublishinghouse.com
E-mail: goodwillpub@vsnl.net
ylp@bol.net.in

Laser typeset at: Computer Corner, New Delhi

Printed at: Kumar Offset, Delhi

Preface

Everyone is not fortunate to be self-employed. Since work is a source of livelihood, the only option is to search for an ideal employer and a good job. Besides reasonable money, it is necessary that the job must provide satisfaction of accomplishing something useful and also provide opportunities for personal growth and an acceptance in the society. Almost one third of adult life is spent at the workplace. It must fulfill personal hopes and aspirations.

Two out of every five persons are not happy with what they are doing. What is worse is that because of personal constraints they are unable to change over to something more satisfying. This results in mediocrity in almost every field of work. Had these people thought of some obvious things when they set out in a career, they would have put their talents and skills to better use and also found greater happiness.

The job market, like everything else, is also changing rapidly. People are moving from one country to another, many activities are now being outsourced in the interests of great efficiency and profitability. Jobs and services are being offered on the Internet. A greater value is being placed on individual skills and abilities. At the same time, there is greater competition for jobs and young people are striving harder to prepare for them through better training and knowledge.

7 Steps to A Super Job takes you step by step into the intricacies of preparing yourself for a career and a job. The book will help you seek the best employer and an ideal job. It also guides you how to apply for a job, prepare an attractive curriculum vitae and be prepared for the interview. It shows you how to develop the skills and abilities that lead to success in a job. When one gives of one's best performance and understands how to work in harmony with the workplace environment, it is not long before it becomes a super job. One learns to find happiness and success in one's job.

— Prem P. Bhalla

CONTENTS

Preparing for a Job

No one really wants to take up a job. If one could have his or her own way, one would like to be the boss of his or her own workplace and follow a routine to suit one's pleasure. Alas, it is not possible. Everyone is not in the position either to have one's own workplace or have the ability and acumen to be one's own boss. Running any kind of organisation requires special skills. This is especially true when the purpose of the organisation is to make a profit and provide livelihood to one or more people.

The only other alternative to make a livelihood is to take up a job in an established organisation and provide services that depend upon one's skills and abilities, and in compensation receive a regular salary. Different jobs require different skills and abilities. In the same way, different people possess different skills and abilities. In an ideal situation, the skills and abilities of a person must be consistent with the skills and abilities required for a particular kind of work. Every entrepreneur makes an effort to get the best persons to fulfill different responsibilities in the organisation. When the matching is proper, the organisation prospers, and so do the people who fulfill the multifarious responsibilities. But this does not always happen.

It is unfortunate that two out of every five people are doing jobs they do not enjoy. Under such circumstances can we expect success? Certainly not! A person who is compelled to do a job more because of circumstances than because of personal happiness and satisfaction one gets from doing something can never be happy doing it. This leads to displeasure for the person and the family. To avoid such a situation in one's life, it is necessary for a person to be well prepared before one takes up a job. Let us study how a person can step ahead to take up a 'super job'.

Begin Early

In some cultures, young people realise it early that they must work to earn a livelihood. This early realisation helps them to take stock of the situation sooner. The majority of young people who live under the shade of their parental protection do not realise early enough that they need to break away from this patronage some day and face the world to make a livelihood. An appropriate selection of a career at the right time can save young people many avoidable frustrations. They can prepare themselves at an early age and gradually move from their teens into responsible adulthood. Several factors are involved in making preparations and in selecting and getting established in a career. Every young person is faced with many questions.

- Why do I need to work?
- How are work and money connected?
- Why is it necessary to be honest?

- What options are available to me to earn a livelihood?
- How can I know what career is best for me?
- Which are the careers that offer the best opportunities?
- Are there enough opportunities in the careers that interest me?
- What skills and abilities would I need to be successful in a career?
- Do I understand the situation well, or are my feelings pushing me towards a particular direction?
- Where can I seek help when I need it?
- How does one plan a career?
- How do I get a good job?
- For how long will I need to work until I can be my own boss?

The answers are not difficult to find. We must understand them to take positive steps towards building a career on a strong foundation. These will help us make appropriate preparations before we are ready to take up a job. Can you add to the common answers one gets to the foregoing questions?

- **The need to work:** Everyone needs to work because it is a source of one's livelihood. Besides money, work can be a great source of personal fulfillment and satisfaction. It leads to an important position in the society. Most people are known by the kind of work they do.

- **Money and work are connected:** Unless one inherits money from the forefathers and decides to live on it, there is no other way to earn money than to work, to fulfill a genuine human need and be paid for it. The harder and smarter a person works, the more money one earns.

- **Money and honesty are related to each other:** Money is a great motivating force for both the good and the bad. It puts a person's honesty and integrity to test. This makes it necessary that if one must benefit from work, one must be honest with self and others.

- **Options to earn a livelihood:** There are innumerable options to earn a livelihood. Although mankind continues to have three basic needs of food, clothing and shelter, these needs have sprouted into an untold number of needs. Each of these needs present opportunities to fulfill them, to build a career upon them.

- **The best career:** It is difficult to tell which career is the best in the world. Every vocational activity aims at fulfilling human needs. All of them are necessary. The money one earns depends upon the interaction of demand and supply. When the demand is greater than the supply, one is paid a higher wage for the same job, and vice versa. A person's efficiency depends upon the satisfaction one derives from work.

Therefore, the best career is one from which one derives the greatest pleasure and fulfilment.

- **Opportunities in careers:** All careers offer opportunities. Since the human mind is fickle and some need change with time and situation, it is necessary to understand the changing trends and to utilize opportunities to one's advantage. The intelligent person does not wait for opportunities. Instead, one creates opportunities by making mankind aware of new and different kinds of needs.

- **Skills and abilities for a career:** Each career requires a set of skills and abilities. To be successful in a career, one must possess these skills and abilities. Nobody is born with all the skills and abilities. These need to be developed through education, training and experience.

- **Personal feelings:** Most young people do not understand the vocational scene. They are often pushed by pressure from the parents, the teachers and the friends. Young people are especially prone to be attracted towards glamour and money in some careers. These can be deceptive and can lead one in the wrong direction.

- **Seeking help:** Most young people turn to those who know them best – their parents, teachers, friends and others for help. In most cases, this advice may not be the best because the person giving it may not be completely aware of the situation. For the best advice, one should seek help from a professional career counsellor.

- **Planning a career:** Just as a well-planned house provides greater comfort and satisfaction, a well-planned career leads one towards success and fulfillment. One must set out to plan a career in early life, and gradually move up the ladder of success in harmony with one's targets.

- **Seeking the right job:** A plan must have a place for everything. Seeking the right job should be a part of the career plan. When it is a part of the many targets you set for yourself, you will gradually move towards the right job.

- **Period of work:** In every field, there is a limitation to the number of years one can work; one is bound by one's health and age. Retirement age is set in many fields, and this cannot be altered. Some people plan to retire before time after saving enough to live comfortably or to do something that gives greater satisfaction and fulfillment rather than money. The time one desires to put at work should be a part of the career plan.

Think it over...

We are told that talent creates its own opportunity. But it sometimes seems that desire creates not only its own opportunities, but its own talents.

— *Eric Hoffer*

Selecting the Right Career

Young people are influenced by several factors when selecting a career. Most of them are not able to differentiate between what is right and what appears to be right. They are also unable to gauge their own strengths and weaknesses and are often swayed towards what is attractive rather than what is useful. One will do well to understand some of the factors that influence career decisions.

- **The glamour of some careers:** Many are attracted by the glamour that is a part of some careers. A career in films, television, politics, modeling, and games and sports always appears attractive to young people. A lot of limelight falls on those who succeed in these fields. Despite the many pitfalls in such careers, glamour clouds their selection.

- **Careers of celebrities:** Most young people look up to celebrities and others known to them who have achieved success and recognition in their field of work. This attraction is more because of the admiration for these people rather than for the skills and abilities that led them to their important positions in life.

- **Attraction to certain fields of activity:** Many are attracted to becoming a doctor or an engineer not because they understand the obligations and responsibilities involved, or because they possess skills and abilities leading to these fields, but because they are fascinated with the kind of work involved in these careers.

- **Parental influence:** The influence of the parents outweighs all others when young people consider various careers. This is because of their dependence upon their parents. Experience has shown that parents are not the best people to guide their children in these matters. It is not that they do not know their children well. Rather they know them best. While they may know the strengths and weaknesses of their children better than others, their judgment may be biased in favour or against certain careers. Besides, few parents have the knowledge or insight pertaining to the vocational scene at a particular time.

- **The influence of teachers:** We cannot ignore the influence that the teachers, consciously or subconsciously, exert upon all young people in search of a suitable career. The influence that the teachers exert comes through stray remarks about a young person's capabilities in certain subjects that lead to a particular career. Since young people are receptive to encouraging remarks, definite inclinations begin to emerge in their fertile minds. Many of such suggestions have been fruitful. However, unless one has received training in vocational guidance or has a reasonable knowledge about various careers, the teacher's suggestions may not always be ideal in selecting a career.

- **The influence of friends:** Many may find it difficult to believe, but young people are greatly influenced by friends not only about common everyday matters but also about the selection of a career. Few realize that their friends are riding the same boat. They are in no better position. The trials and tribulations of adolescence make young people emotionally sensitive. Under such circumstances, it may not at all be advisable to rely upon the counsel of friends who may be facing similar problems. Friends can do no better than help point out one's strengths and weaknesses. This may be useful to analyse one's feelings and attitudes about a particular career. Friend's parents can provide some guidance pertaining to the vocations and businesses they are personally pursuing in their everyday life.

- **Discussions, magazines and books:** Some serious-minded young people are influenced by discussions at school or in other spheres, by the magazines and books on vocational guidance and various careers that they may be encouraged to read. In such situations, since young people lack confidence to make firm decisions, they need to be helped by parents, teachers and others.

- **Career counseling:** Many schools, colleges and universities have established vocational guidance centres. Some invite professional counselors to advise the students. Vocational guidance officers are attached to some employment exchanges. The vocational counselors do not have a secret formula that can lead a young person to choose a suitable career. Their role is to guide young people to explore personal feelings, skills and abilities as are required to pursue particular careers. They encourage young people to search for answers within themselves, rather than be lectured at, as most parents and teachers tend to do. Vocational counselors can provide useful information on occupational trends at a particular time.

Think it over...

The things taught in schools and colleges are not education, but means of an education.

— *Ralph W. Emerson*

Basic Education

There was a time when a person just needed to be able to read and write, and one learnt as one gained experience in a career. People learnt skills as they grew slowly at the workplace. For many careers, just eight years of study in a school were considered sufficient. It is not so today. Irrespective of the skills a person may learn, a minimum of a pass in high school is necessary. Those who possess skills may not immediately agree with this minimum requirement, but it has been repeatedly experienced that when it comes to promotions and growth, despite one's skills, a good basic education is necessary. Those who possess it are preferred because education broadens one's outlook and enables one to see ahead. A good basic education is an asset in every career.

What constitutes a good education is a debatable point. One sees many young people chasing degrees in the hope that it will get them closer to a good job. One comes across many young men and women who are graduates and postgraduates applying for jobs that do not need a college education.

A good basic education should lead a young person to learn how to find personal fulfillment in a career of one's choice. It should help one to develop an appreciation of life in its true form. In general, a basic education of the higher secondary level prepares all young people for adult life. Beyond this all those inclined towards academics should pursue higher education in a subject of their choice, and others should learn skills that lead them to particular careers where they can find fulfillment. To evaluate your progress, answer these simple questions:

- Have you done well in your studies to the higher secondary level? If not, why?

- Have you been able to short-list careers of your choice? If not, when will you do it?
- Have you prepared plans to acquire the necessary skills and abilities for the careers you have in mind? Have you made a written outline of the plans?
- Did you think, plan and choose the subjects for the +2 level? Was your choice right?
- Were you able to choose the best courses of study beyond the 10+2 level? Will they lead you to the career of your choice?
- Does the study plan include practical training? Whenever available it is an asset to finding a good job.

Vocational Training

One must have relevant knowledge about one's job before it is possible to succeed. One cannot rise in a career without adequate preparation. We are living in an age of specialization where one must be well equipped for a variety of situations. If all young people would understand the need for acquiring requisite knowledge and skills, the all round efficiency would rise and people would experience much greater fulfillment in their jobs.

Millions of people all over the world are doing the same jobs, which they were doing ten or more years ago. There is a significant difference in that people are striving to be more efficient than ever before. All human endeavour aims at increasing efficiency. If it were not so, we would be where we were hundreds of years ago. Each generation takes over where the last one leaves. This could be possible only by upgrading knowledge and providing vocational training to benefit the new entrants beginning a career.

Young people who have received vocational training are in a better position to find a job than those who have overlooked it. Employers are interested in young people who have the basic knowledge about their career. When compared to a person with some experience, but no training, a trained person has better prospects of not only matching with experience but also surpassing it soon.

Vocational training is superior to collecting degrees in arts or science subjects, unless these are specifically required for a particular career. For example, young people who are trained in fields like leather technology, hotel management, or catering management after completing school have better prospects of finding a job than those who may have done degree courses in different languages or in subjects like Economics and Political Science.

In a nation like India, which has a vast population of young people, the facilities for vocational training do not always match demand. Generally, there is great competition to find admission in these institutions. To control the demand, competitive examinations are held for admission. Since these exams are not always based upon the school curriculum, even when a person is capable and has been doing well in school, one may fail to qualify. It is advisable to plan ahead of time. One must look out for institutions that offer courses of interest, get the prospectus and application forms, and prepare ahead for the special admission tests.

It is important to know the entrance requirements, period of study, diploma or degree awarded, job training provided after the course, hostel facilities, the cost of education, and other such pertinent information about the course and the institution. It is useful to collect information from as many institutions as possible because that provides an opportunity to compare the courses and the facilities offered by the institutions. It may not be possible to get admission in the institution of one's choice, but with choices available, one can select the institution that offers the maximum benefits. Applications for admission can then be made well in time.

Think it over...

My idea of education is to unsettle the minds of the young and inflame their intellects.

— *Robert M. Hutchins*

Institutions of Higher Education

Most young people seeking admission in institutions of higher learning are at a loss about the preparation required for admission. They are not aware of the institutions that offer courses that would lead them towards the career of their choice. Several publishers have published directories that give details of the institutions that offer courses in a particular field. Advertisements in the national newspapers, regional newspapers and also the local newspapers can also be very helpful. Many school and college libraries stock these directories. They are handy guides to locate institutions for higher education.

Besides the popular colleges and universities listed in the directories, there are many private educational institutions and universities that offer a variety of courses and also provide vocational training. The details of the institutions nearest to you can be had from the State Education Department or from the directories published by the government. Several voluntary organisations also provide vocational training. Many private institutions advertise in the local and national press. Young people interested in courses offered by them will do well to obtain the necessary information directly.

Financing Higher Education

Higher education has become expensive. Unable to meet the rising costs, even the government is encouraging private institutions to provide education. Since the emphasis in private institutions is on quality and appropriate placements for the students on completion of the courses, the college fee is on the higher side, and it is increasing each year. With dependence upon parents, the cost of education is an important consideration to all young people. Almost no facilities for working and studying together are available, except in a few special cases.

Young people who are confident of their abilities can take advantage of the financial help offered by banks at reasonable rates of interest. For the exceptionally brilliant students, many charitable trusts offer scholarships and loans. The government also offers scholarships to brilliant students. The details can be had from the booklets published by the government from time to time. They can be purchased from booksellers who stock government publications. The details of scholarships and other aids available at the college level can be had directly from the institutions concerned, or from the District Inspector of Schools.

Making up for Educational Deficiencies

Compelled by personal circumstances many young people take up jobs without sufficient knowledge or training, hoping that they will make up for the deficiency over a period through on-the-job experience. This experience is certainly useful, but it is not a substitute for formal vocational education and training. Many argue that formal training is more theoretical than practical. It has been observed that formal vocational training provides many details, which may appear insignificant, but in actual practice provide the very foundation to practical success. Once a young person is equipped with this knowledge, steady progress becomes a part of the career.

Fortunately, to make up for this deficiency, many educational institutions are now offering short-term courses. For the convenience of working people, many of these are offered as evening classes. Where such facilities are not easily available, one can still study the theoretical aspects of the subject through distance education. Many universities are preparing young people for degree courses, and for special examinations conducted by professional organizations. Diploma courses are also offered. Special courses that extend over a week or fortnight are offered by some institutions, especially for those engaged in particular trades. Vocational knowledge is very important to rise in one's career. One must update knowledge to be relevant and grow in the present times.

Distance Education

Many education boards and universities have open schools that offer facilities for education through correspondence. This has its own advantages in that one can study according to one's personal convenience, making it possible to earn and learn simultaneously. The education imparted is simple and worthwhile, but lacks the discipline of attending regular classes. To succeed, one must work diligently and have self-control. Most employers recognize the degrees and diplomas awarded by universities and important correspondence schools. One must choose the course that would be beneficial in one's personal circumstances and work towards success.

Think it over...

Personality is an indefinable thing, a strange force that has power over souls of men.

— *Jawaharlal Nehru*

Personality Traits

Most young people are not able to analyse their feelings and attitudes to draw a clear picture of their personality. They may know how they feel but may not be able to express their feelings in words or on paper, to define their personal image. A qualified psychologist is the best person to assist young people to identify areas of strength and weakness, and clearly define personality traits.

Since the services of a psychologist are not readily available to young people, there is an alternative way to identify one's personality traits. Given below is a list of words that describe common personality traits and feelings found in people. The list is fairly exhaustive. Some more traits could be added, but the common ones are there. English has a large vocabulary. There are several words that appear to have similar meaning. However, each word has finer meanings. You can choose ones that describe you best. Tick those that describe your feelings. Ignore those that do not relate to you. If you are not sure of the meaning of a word, consult a dictionary. The words are in alphabetic order. They describe both the strengths and weaknesses in people. Irrespective of that, tick those that describe you best.

Absent-minded	Adaptable	Aesthetic	Affectionate
Aggressive	Alert	Ambitious	Amiable
Anxious	Apprehensive	Arrogant	Artistic
Assertive	Attractive	Authoritarian	Autocratic
Beautiful	Boastful	Boisterous	Bold
Brave	Broadminded	Calm	Candid
Capable	Careless	Cautious	Charitable
Charming	Cheerful	Childish	Clumsy
Committed	Companionable	Compassionate	Competent
Complaining	Composed	Compulsive	Conceited
Confident	Conformist	Confused	Conscientious
Considerate	Contented	Convincing	Coolheaded
Co-operative	Cordial	Courageous	Courteous
Crazy	Creative	Critical	Crude
Cruel	Curt	Daring	Decisive
Dependable	Depressed	Detached	Devoted
Dictatorial	Diligent	Diplomatic	Disciplined

Discouraged	Discreet	Dishonest	Disillusioned
Disinterested	Docile	Dominant	Dramatic
Dreamy	Dull	Dutiful	Eager
Easily-hurt	Easy-going	Egoistic	Emotional
Encouraging	Enthusiastic	Erratic	Ethical
Evasive	Excitable	Failure	Faint-hearted
Fair	Faithful	Far-sighted	Fashionable
Fearful	Feeble	Fickle	Firm
Flamboyant	Flexible	Flimsy	Foolish
Forgiving	Formal	Frail	Friendly
Gaudy	Generous	Gentle	Genuine
Good-looking	Gorgeous	Graceful	Greedy
Gullible	Half-hearted	Handicapped	Handsome
Hardboiled	Hard-headed	Hardy	Haughty
Headstrong	Healthy	Helpful	Hesitant
Honest	Humane	Humble	Humorous
Hypocritical	Idealistic	Ignorant	Imaginative
Immature	Impartial	Impulsive	Inattentive
Incompetent	Indifferent	Indulgent	Industrious
Inefficient	Ingenious	Insensitive	Insincere

Intellectual	Interfering	Inventive	Jittery
Just	Knowledgeable	Lavish	Lazy
Lenient	Liberal	Lively	Lonely
Loving	Magnanimous	Mature	Maudlin
Mean	Meek	Mellow	Merciful
Methodical	Meticulous	Mischievous	Moody
Motivated	Negative	Negligent	Nervous
Novel	Objective	Observant	Obstinate
Offensive	Officious	Orderly	Original
Ostentatious	Outspoken	Partisan	Patient
Pedantic	Performer	Persevering	Persistent
Persuasive	Pious	Placid	Plain
Pleasant	Polite	Positive	Precise
Pretty	Procrastinating	Proud	Prudent
Puerile	Pushing	Rash	Rational
Reasonable	Refined	Religious	Reluctant
Reserved	Resourceful	Responsible	Rigid
Romantic	Rude	Sacrificing	Saucy
Scrupulous	Secure	Self-confident	Self-conscious
Selfish	Sensible	Sensitive	Sentimental

Serene	Sharp	Shrewd	Shy
Simpleton	Sincere	Slavish	Sloppy
Slow	Smart	Smug	Sober
Sociable	Sophisticated	Spirited	Spiteful
Spontaneous	Sporting	Steady	Stern
Straightforward	Strict	Strong-willed	Stupid
Suave	Subjective	Submissive	Subservient
Successful	Superficial	Supportive	Suspicious
Sympathetic	Tactful	Talkative	Tame
Theatrical	Thoughtful	Thoughtless	Timid
Tolerant	Tough	Tranquil	Trendy
Trusting	Truthful	Unassuming	Unbiased
Uncertain	Unconcerned	Undisciplined	Undisturbed
Unethical	Unruffled	Upright	Vain
Versatile	Vindictive	Virtuous	Vivacious
Volatile	Vulgar	Wasteful	Weak-willed
Well-behaved	Wile	Winning	Witty
Worldly	Worrier	Zealous	

After you have gone through the list and ticked the ones that describe you best, note down the words that you have ticked. Do it honestly in privacy. These words describe you and your feelings. Sort them in two groups. The first list should include words that describe your strengths. The second list should include words that describe your weaknesses. You can differentiate between the two by asking yourself what is the effect of the particular trait. If it contributes to your confidence, it is a positive trait. It adds to your strength. If it robs you of your confidence, it is a weakness. Together the two lists will help you describe and understand yourself better.

Think it over...

The winds and waves are always on the side of the ablest navigators.

— *Edward Gibbon*

Abilities That Lead to Success

Every job requires a set of abilities and skills. Success is not possible without them. Besides, those who possess those abilities and skills enjoy the work. Others just drag their way through work. Since every individual is unique, the abilities and skills too vary from one person to another. Some abilities and skills come naturally. Others need to be learnt. This learning too depends upon individual preferences.

Listed below are abilities and skills that promote success in a variety of careers. Tick ones that you possess. Later, compare these with the desirable qualities that are necessary in particular careers. If you lack certain skills, you can make up through appropriate training.

Ability to comfort people

Ability to handle crises

Ability to make decisions

Ability to see in graphic form

- Above average creativity
- Adaptable to changing circumstances
- All-round knowledge
- Analytical outlook
- Appreciate discipline in life
- Appreciate need for secrecy
- Appreciate composition and colour
- Can face stress and tension
- Communication skills
- Computer literacy
- Enjoy self-confidence
- Enjoy working with numbers
- Enjoy working with machines
- Fond of reading
- Fond of upgrading skills
- Get along well with people
- Good etiquette and manners
- Good health and physique
- Good imagination
- Good knowledge of one's field
- Good language skills
- Good leadership qualities
- Good listening skills
- Good memory for names and faces
- Good observation
- Good speaking skills
- Good team member
- Good writing skills
- Have an eye for unscrupulous people
- High intellectual ability
- Highly quality conscious
- Highly self-motivated

Integrity and honour	Love for adventure and fun
Love for animals	Love for nature and outdoors
Not easily discouraged	Pleasing personality
Possess an aesthetic sense	Possess special artistic skills
Ready to work with own hands	Respect for time
Sense of showmanship	Sensitive to others' problems
Sincere and service-minded	Thorough and methodical
Understands shapes and figures	Vision to see ahead
Willing to take responsibility	Willing to try new ideas
Willing to work in different locations	Willing to work late at odd hours

Personal Feelings

No young person can ignore personal feelings about a career and still be successful in it. Everyone must be aware of one's hopes, aspirations and personal preferences. The process of self-analysis must be ruthlessly realistic. You can be dishonest with somebody else and get away with it. When one's future is involved, one personally suffers for it. Therefore, one must always analyse personal feelings in strict honesty.

To understand your feelings, abilities and skills, note down everything on paper. Here are a few questions. The answers will tell you much about you.

- Do your family circumstances permit you to take up the career you have in mind?
- Have you been able to list your strengths and weaknesses? How do you rate yourself?
- Is your basic education adequate? Are you working to acquire the knowledge that would be necessary for the job you have in mind?
- How do you rate your study habits, considering the time spent for the purpose each day? What newspapers, magazines and books do you read?
- How do you rate your health? Are you prone to ailments like coughs and cold? Will health influence your selection of a job?
- Do you make friends quickly, or do you prefer relationships with a few reliable friends?
- Can you develop your strengths further, and use them in your career?
- Can you overcome your limitations? How and by when?
- Will your hobbies be useful to you in your career?
- Is your attitude in harmony with the capabilities required for the career of your choice?

- Are you physically and emotionally ready to meet the challenges that the career will offer?

Think about the answers to these questions. Take your time over them. Give due thought to every aspect of your requirements. The correct picture will soon emerge before you.

Think it over...

A distorted view of one's abilities can make it hard to cope with the real world.

— *Alison Gardner*

Understanding Yourself

Personal evaluation aims at a person being able to identify one's strengths, sensitivities and shortcomings. When you consider the many unseen influences that affect you and answer questions relating to your own feelings, personality traits, interests and abilities, you are able to understand yourself completely.

Assess your strengths and shortcomings to draw an honest picture of you. You will do well to consider your family status and reputation, your personal appearance and physique, the availability of a personal conveyance, or other similar considerations. You will also need to consider personal sensitivities, lack of confidence, religious restrictions, secret fears, and other similar shortcomings.

Whatever be the image that emerges from answering the questions would reflect the person you are. Use the information as a stepping stone to a job and career of your choice. Do not let the shortcomings discourage you. Your ability to have identified them means that you are aware of them and can get over them. Having identified your real self, you are at an advantage to evaluate the career opportunities open to you. You will be able to select a career of your choice.

Points to Ponder...

- When a person cannot be self-employed, the only option is to take up a job.
- One must begin early to prepare oneself for a career.
- Selecting the right career is a critical choice in one's life. One must consider all the aspects before taking the decision.
- A good basic education is the foundation of a satisfying career.
- Young people who have received vocational training are in a better position to find a good job.
- One must prepare well ahead of time to take admission into institutions of higher learning.
- Higher education is becoming more expensive each day.
- One can make up for educational deficiencies by joining short-term courses.
- Distance education has opened up frontiers for young people who need to work and study simultaneously.

- Young people must evaluate their strengths and weaknesses before finally taking up a career.

- It is useful to match one's abilities with those required for a career of your choice.

- Evaluate the situation thoroughly before making the final decision of a career.

- Understand your own hopes and aspirations to get ahead in life.

Seeking the Best Job

Everyone seeking the best job is really in search for the best employer and an ideal working environment. It is good to have such a target before oneself, but many question whether such a person and circumstances really exist. Besides, before one can really find the best employer, it is necessary that he must have an appropriate job to offer. We have earlier discussed that two out of every five persons are in jobs that they do not like. Under such circumstances, can these people ever be efficient? Can we expect them to put in their best in a job they do not like? When a person cannot put in his or her best in a job, how much can the employer gain from such work?

Every person seeking a job is looking for two things. First, the kind of work that is in harmony with one's personality. Besides a livelihood, everyone seeks fulfillment through work. It is this fulfillment that motivates people to work harder and be effective. Second, everyone desires that the employer must be a kind and understanding person. In the larger companies and organisations, an employee does not directly come into contact with the employer through work because the shareholders own the company. However, the boss who oversees one's work represents the employer.

One can always set out to seek something. To be able to get it is quite another. Job profiles never come tailor-made. They depend upon what the employer is in search of and how he desires to attain it. Since different people can employ different methods to attain the same thing, job profiles and responsibilities can vary greatly from one place to another. We cannot also overlook that employers are human beings and like all others are subject to idiosyncrasies that are hard to explain. Everyone will behave in his or her own peculiar way. It may suit some and not others. Let us take a closer look at the situation.

Job Opportunities

Most young people grumble about the lack of good job opportunities. In reality, they do not know what a job opportunity is. One needs to understand that job opportunities come as human needs. Wherever there are people, there will be needs to be fulfilled. A job opportunity is no more than being able to recognize human needs, and then satisfying them for certain remuneration. Every working person is doing this. One may be doing it through a job while another may be self-employed. It is immaterial whether one is working in a home, or in a factory, field or office. The remuneration a person gets for work represents the price for labour to satisfy a particular human need.

The office executive satisfies the need for management of the resources. The accountant looks after the finances. The office staff provides clerical, record keeping and other similar services. The workers in the factory keep up the manufacturing schedule. Every person contributes his or her little bit to fulfill the need of producing the final product that ultimately satisfies the need of the consumer. Products and services vary, but the basic truth is that opportunities for gainful employment begin with human needs.

These needs are often very complex. An observant person may recognize a special need and convinced of its remunerative value, may convert it into an opportunity for gainful employment for self and others. Through a person's effort many more may benefit. Several people may contribute their labour by doing jobs as varied as extracting the raw material to selling the finished product in retail. One human need leads to another. When people begin to recognize human needs, they learn how to convert them into opportunities for gainful employment for themselves.

Understanding Human Needs

The life of the prehistoric man rotated around three principle needs - food, clothing and shelter. With time, as mankind became more organized, other needs grew out of the basic needs. Enterprising men and women looked at these needs as opportunities for gainful employment for themselves. Surprisingly, human needs continue to grow. Mankind existed for thousands of years without many of the services and products we enjoy today. Nobody missed anything. Today we cannot think of a life without them. They seem vital to our existence. These needs must find fulfillment.

Many of the human needs are not easy to recognize. Only the observant few have set forth to understand the latent needs of mankind. These have provided opportunities to find gainful employment. For example, the need for clothing is a simple basic human need. However, it was observed that wearing any kind of clothes does not provide complete satisfaction. People desire comfort and variety. They want to look different from one another. They are in search for better fabrics and designs.

Because of these simple observations, millions of young people have found work preparing raw materials like cotton, wool, silk and manmade fibres, processing them, creating new designs, fashioning them into attractive garments, and eventually reaching the customers through a network of sales outlets throughout the world. As the consumer becomes more conscious about garment designs and trends in fashion, the opportunities to produce better fabrics and garments continue to grow.

The basic human needs are only food, clothing and shelter. Innumerable needs have emerged from these three. These offer gainful employment to millions of people in every sphere of life. The need for entertainment alone has created opportunities for theatres, circuses, tourism, a huge film and TV industry, sports and a whole lot of other things to keep mankind free from boredom. Books and magazines are not only educative but are a source of entertainment also, and this opportunity has created millions of jobs in a vast publishing network that is spread around the world. Hundreds of thousands of magazines and books are published each year.

The human need to look attractive has given rise to a multimillion cosmetic industry, which has provided gainful employment to millions of people all over the world. Can you estimate the number of men and women who are running beauty parlours? Many human needs appear unimportant. Yet, enterprising people have used them to build big business concerns. For example, the need to convey a simple message with a touch of humour has given rise to a huge business of publishing greeting and business cards. These have found ready acceptance by millions of people because they help connect people with the least effort. These have made it possible to reach out in a variety of circumstances.

Human nature is fickle. We want something on one occasion and quite another at a different time. To understand human needs, one should be observant and analytical. While the basic needs for food, clothing and shelter continue to be the same as they were for the primitive man, to these we can add the need for health, happiness and security. Millions of people have found gainful employment through these human needs and will continue to do so as long as man lives on this planet.

Think it over...

Where there is more opportunity there is usually more ambition, and where there is more ambition there is an incentive to effort and improvement.

— *C.D. Deshmukh*

Opportunities are Growing

Each time a new discovery is made, an invention perfected, or a new product or service marketed, most young people feel discouraged that yet another opportunity is exhausted. This is not true. Each opportunity used opens up newer opportunities for gainful employment of people. Look back at the time when some of the most commonly used household products like fountain pens, bicycles, radios, telephones, record players or other similar articles were first put up for sale. Each one of these products was acclaimed as the ultimate in ingenuity and human endeavour.

When we look at any one of these today, we find that the present models resemble the original very slightly, and yet the efficiency is manifold. At one time these items were new to mankind. However, each of these items has opened new opportunities for millions of young people. The original product or service has not only been improved, but it is now being manufactured and marketed at prices that have enabled more people to buy them. Millions of people around the world are busy manufacturing, selling and maintaining these products. A large number is engaged in making improvisations because the stage of perfection is still a distant dream.

New human needs are discovered each day. These are opportunities for gainful employment. Products and services sold in one community or country are waiting to be introduced into new areas. Scientific knowledge and experience are growing. The fruits of this labour are waiting to be utilized for the welfare of mankind. The people around the world have a variety of needs and preferences. Each of these continues to offer untold possibilities for fulfillment, and in return providing gainful employment.

Evaluating Opportunities

One needs to be realistic in evaluating opportunities for employment. We cannot afford to ignore facts because of personal sentiments and prejudices. It is not always possible to be completely original about providing so-called new products and services. We stand where we are today because of the improvisations each generation has made over what we inherited from our forefathers. There has always got to be a first time. What do we lose by copying an idea, or introducing something that does not exist in our community?

Making improvements in existing products and services is an unlimited source of opportunities leading to gainful employment. Many of the products and services we enjoy today are really based on ideas given to us many, many years ago by people we do not even know about today. In evaluating opportunities, let us not overlook some simple observations.

- **Opportunities are growing:** Opportunities for gainful employment are not becoming scarce. They are growing in direct proportion to the population.

- **Creating opportunities:** An opportunity is a favourable combination of circumstances, time and place.

- **Different point of view:** Every person looks at a product, service or an opportunity from his or her point of view. This depends upon one's knowledge, experience and the insight developed over a period.

- **Personal satisfaction:** Opportunities for employment must not be evaluated on the basis of the human needs they fulfill or the remuneration that is offered, but on the basis of the personal satisfaction it offers.

- **Dignity of labour:** Personal fulfillment in a job depends greatly upon one's concept of dignity of labour. Unless one's attitudes are in harmony with the labour required in a particular kind of work, one cannot find satisfaction.

- **The level of competition:** One should not be discouraged by the level of competition that exists in a particular field of work. Competition is not an obstacle but rather a challenge. Do not forget that the level of competition is the same for everyone.

Besides, if there is competition, it means that the possibilities in the field are attractive to many.

- **Opportunities within competition:** Have you observed that even within competition there are opportunities for gainful employment? Coaching institutes are helping young people learn how to be competitive.

- **Ignore "pulls and pushes":** Many young people complain about their lack in being able to "pull or push" their way to gainful employment. This is a wrong attitude to have. Use your own abilities and skills to push ahead. Leave the rest to God.

Think it over...

Modern planning has as its major theme the desire of man to control his own destiny.

— *Stephen Grabow*

Planning the Career

Planning is the key to success. Without it, one can go astray. Governments plan in terms of five-year plans. Organisations plan to attain several kinds of goals. Individuals make plans in terms of personal hopes and aspirations. Planning is not only about setting and attaining goals. There are many things that need consideration. One needs to look at resources, the prevalent circumstances, what needs to be achieved, when it needs to be achieved, how it needs to be achieved, what obstacles could hinder progress, and how can one utilize the available resources usefully? The answers to these questions simplify the making of a plan.

Careers are planned in a similar way. One cannot afford to leave matters to chance or luck. One must deliberately plan one's destiny. To do so one will need to evaluate personal hopes, aspirations and resources. Using this information as the starting point, one must decide upon the kind of work one would like to do. A focussed mind provides a sense of direction and helps one move towards the goal.

One can begin with collecting data about the career one desires to pursue. The next step would be preparing oneself for challenges that are a part of all kinds of careers. A determined attitude helps shape thoughts, plans and actions. These will take you in the right direction. Once a strong foundation is laid, the superstructure that one builds will also be strong. Despite the problems and obstacles that may temporarily delay progress, you will be well on your way to settle in a career of your choice.

Preparing the Plan

To prepare a plan for a career, answer the following questions:

- ❖ Have I evaluated my personality traits, abilities and strengths objectively? How can I use these to develop a career for myself?
- ❖ Have I been able to identify my shortcomings and weaknesses? Can I get over them? If so, by when can I do it?
- ❖ Considering my abilities and circumstances what career choices are open to me? Have I short-listed the best of them to 3 choices? What are they?

- Have I been able to collect the details about the careers that I have short-listed? Considering the details, can I prioritize them as first, second and third?

- Has it been possible to identify the institutions that can help me prepare for the three careers I have short-listed? Can I fulfill their admission and other requirements?

- What will be the financial requirements for training in the institutions of my choice? From where will these requirements be met?

- What are the job prospects after the training? Have I checked with the old students who have passed from these institutions? Is there any campus recruitment?

Write the answers to the questions on paper. A clear picture of the situation will begin to emerge. You will begin to see the direction towards which you will need to move. The facts before you will help you prepare a plan to take you towards your goal.

The Right Career

Have you observed the order in a planned city and confusion in a city that has grown haphazardly? Have you observed how people live in skyscrapers, in huge buildings, in bungalows and also in huts and shanties? All these provide the security of a home to many families. Some provide comfort and security; others just provide a shelter from the vagaries of nature. The difference lies in planning that begins with a thought and progresses towards the goal taking into consideration all kinds of details in building a superstructure and incorporating useful conveniences and comforts.

Just as one plans a building beginning with a thought, one proceeds towards choosing the right career also beginning with a thought. What would you like to do? Let the thought occupy the mind until you feel it is just the thing you would like to pursue. You would want your career to be established on a strong foundation. Collect all the information you can about it. Talk to people who are already engaged in that field of careers. Ask for information from friends and others. Read books about it in the library. Do not be fascinated with the remuneration that may appear tempting or by the prestige and glamour that make some careers attractive.

Answer these questions honestly to appreciate the situation better. Are you aware of the obligations and responsibilities of the career you would like to take up? What are the minimum educational requirements? Is some practical work-experience necessary before employment? Do you see jobs pertaining to careers in the field regularly advertised in the newspapers? Do you anticipate special challenges in taking up a career in that field?

Collect as much information as you can from whatever sources available to you. Note it down on paper. Most young people simultaneously consider several careers. When tabulated, the information is useful to narrow down the choice to two or three choices that can then be studied in still greater detail.

With the details of the careers available and you having understood the obligations and responsibilities involved, you can prioritize them giving preference to one that is in harmony with your personality. You will need to consider whether you have the necessary resources to pursue it. One should finalize the choice of a career as early as possible. Once this is done, one knows which way the energy must be directed. One can also begin early to equip oneself through the best education and training.

Think it over...

Everything in this world is possible to the man who knows his job.

— D. Whealey

Looking for a Job

Young people looking for a job would like to seek all the possible choices that are available at any one particular time. This is not easy. It is, therefore, advisable that one should keep on the lookout for a suitable position. Listed below are ways to look out for a job:

- **Campus recruitments:** Many employers are now moving directly to college campuses and recruiting employees on the basis of their performance at the training level. Employers compete with each other to get the best persons to fulfill their exact requirements.

- **Advertisements in newspapers:** One can get to know about the complete range of employment opportunities available by going through the important newspapers every day. Much of advertising space, both in the display and the classified sections, is utilized for providing information about job vacancies. The private sector and the government departments advertise their requirements in the regional and national press.

- **Employment News:** The Directorate of Advertising and Visual Publicity, New Delhi, publishes a weekly paper that covers a wide range of employment opportunities simultaneously in English, Hindi, Bengali, Urdu, Tamil, Telegu and Assamese. Young people in search for a good opening will do well to read it regularly.

- **Trade journals:** We have trade journals in every field of work. For jobs in specialized fields one would do well to look out for advertisements in these journals.

- **The local library:** It may not be possible to simultaneously subscribe to many newspapers and magazines, which carry the 'situations vacant' advertisements. In such circumstances, one could keep in touch with newspapers and other publications at the local library, making personal notes when necessary.

- **The local employment exchange:** One can get oneself registered at the local employment exchange. They will get in touch whenever there is an enquiry from prospective employers.

- **Direct contact with employers:** When a person has special abilities that would interest only a selected number of employers and it is known that the number of employers in that field is limited, one can write directly to the prospective employers informing about the availability of one's services. If a position is not available at that time, it is customary for the employers to keep such applications on file and revert back later. Many such applications have resulted in worthwhile jobs.

- **Job websites:** With everyone becoming computer savvy, it is common for people to post their résumés on popular websites visited by employers. Since many of the applicants are already holding jobs, and do this to move to greener pastures, the websites ensure secrecy when desired.

- **Competitive examinations:** For entry to many jobs as those in the government, the armed forces, and several other fields, where the demand for jobs far exceeds the availability of positions, one needs to qualify in written examinations followed by an interview or other tests.

Jobs through Competitive Examinations

There is a great rush for jobs in several fields of service. Out of necessity, the entry is restricted through competitive examinations. Everyone gets an equal opportunity to appear for a written examination, which automatically eliminates weaker candidates, permitting only the best to come up for the final selection through interviews, personality tests, medical checkups, etc. This form of recruitment has become a regular feature for many fields of service at the state and national level. Jobs in the administrative services, foreign services, police services, defence services, revenue services, the railways and a whole lot of other fields are given on the basis of proficiency checked through competitive examinations. The recruitment to many jobs at the lower cadre like clerks and inspectors are also through similar competitive examinations that are duly advertised in the national press.

Many of the competitive examinations are held just once a year. Thousands of candidates sit for the written tests in examination centres spread all over the country. Those interested in jobs offered through competitive examinations should be well prepared. Applications must be filed as soon as the particular examination is announced in the national press. Besides the important newspapers, the details of these examinations are published in magazines like Employment News, Competition and Success Review, Careers in Science, and other similar publications. Copies of these magazines are available in most college libraries and sold freely at bookstalls.

The examination follows a set well-laid pattern year after year. The candidates must prepare for it thoroughly. Model test papers and guides of all descriptions for these examinations are available in the market. Their huge sale is a clear indication of how the candidates are in search for short cuts to success. Coaching institutions of all kinds have sprung up in almost every town and city in the country. They assure complete guidance to succeed in the examination. Though the coaching institutes help candidates to focus their mind in a definite direction and the test papers and guides prepare one to understand the pattern of the examination, the ultimate success depends upon an individual's capabilities and efforts. Those who have a broad outlook and a good general knowledge of the happenings around them attain success in these examinations.

Think it over...

It is inevitable when one has a great need of something one finds it. What you need you attract like a lover.

— *Gertrude Stein*

Understanding Job Requirements

The purpose of all jobs is the same – to fulfill a human need. The financial gain to the employer may not come directly as the result of the activities of an employee. It may represent one link in a chain of activities where people perform different activities at different levels to produce a product or service that fulfills a human need and also brings in profit to the employer. In itself, the contribution of one person may seem insignificant, but as a part of the chain every role is important to produce the final product or service. With one link becoming weak, the whole process can fail.

In looking for a job, one should remember that while it is important to the prospective employee because his or her livelihood will depend upon it, it is especially important to the employer. Unless the employees fulfill their responsibilities that benefit him, his purpose of hiring employees will be defeated.

When you come across an advertisement that offers a job opportunity that you feel you can fill, the first thing you need to do is to understand the job requirements. Because of expensive space, most advertisements need to be brief and to the point. They do not always provide complete information for prospective candidates to assess the situation. Ask yourself what the advertiser expects to be done. The answers to these questions will lead you to the correct direction.

- Does the advertisement place any restrictions on the age of the applicants?
- What basic educational qualifications does the advertiser desire?

- Is any working experience required?
- Where would the advertiser like you to work?
- Will the job require moving of house or break present family bonds?
- Is residential accommodation available in the area of work?
- What is the salary offered?

After answering these questions, if you feel that you cannot give the job the best of yourself, it is best to forget about it right away. Only if you feel that you have understood the job requirements as desired by the advertiser and can fulfill them efficiently and conveniently, you should apply for the job. It is important that the employer must get the best you can offer. It is equally necessary that you find personal fulfillment from doing a job well. That ensures continued success.

The Ideal Employer

Every employee looks forward to find an ideal employer who can offer the maximum benefits and security of service. The choice is often very limited. One could only look forward to mutually benefit each other so that both the employer and the employee find reasonable satisfaction from the job.

Generally, the employers are categorized according to what they offer by way of working conditions, pay scales, security of service, fringe benefits, bonus, etc. The enactment of several laws pertaining to employment has made the position of employees secure in the sphere of work. The employers are expected to provide several other benefits. Nevertheless, the human factor cannot be ignored. It is the kind of employer-employee relationship which helps differentiate good and bad employers or employees. In an ideal relationship, an employee is treated as an individual personality and not as another machine or piece of equipment in a huge set-up, working from 8 a.m. to 5 p.m.

Given a choice most people prefer jobs in the government departments because they offer the maximum security of service. In comparison with other jobs, they have their own advantages and shortcomings. One needs to weigh them according to one's personal preferences. With general awareness about being effective and with the introduction of computers in every field, there is a trend towards fewer workers and jobs. The entry into these jobs is through competitive examinations. Educational qualifications and merit are important. The general policy in most government departments is to streamline the working and cut down on new jobs.

The large corporate houses offer better pay scales and benefits to employees as compared to the smaller ones, but the responsibility shared is much less and one gains experience gradually. In a smaller concern, though the salary is less, a young person is entrusted with greater responsibility. One gets a good on-the-job experience that gives the person the confidence to handle responsibility independently. This experience and confidence is a useful qualification that helps one get promoted when the right opening emerges.

Whenever a specialist is required to fulfill a responsibility, the larger and the smaller companies pay similar salaries. The top-of-the-line jobs are offered only by the larger concerns. These require a very high degree of knowledge and experience, a sense of responsibility, and complete dedication. Only exceptionally qualified young people make it to these positions. Most young people aspire for lower and middle level jobs.

Points to Ponder...

- Those seeking the best job are really looking for an ideal employer.
- Job opportunities emerge from human needs.
- Understanding human needs is a complex activity.
- Every opportunity used opens the way for newer opportunities.
- One must be realistic in evaluating opportunities for employment.
- Planning is crucial for a successful career.
- Choosing the right career is a crucial choice for every young person.
- One must look for job opportunities in the right places.
- Several kinds of jobs are available through competitive examinations.
- It is necessary to understand job requirements before applying for it.
- Good employer-employee relationships begin with cordial human relationships.

Applying for the Job

When a person has acquired the basic education and also prepared to take up a job in a particular field, it is time to get in touch with the prospective employers. Jobs through competitive examinations involve making applications for a particular examination. These applications are usually on prescribed forms where the details need to be filled. Anyone with common sense can do it well. No special preparation or knowledge is required.

Campus recruitments involve interviews and assessment on the basis of one's college record and abilities and skills of prospective candidates as assessed by the teachers. However, this would be the first job. Unless there is harmony between the employer and the employee, which is possible only when everything fits in well, one is likely to change jobs and the skills necessary for applying for a job would be necessary then.

It is unfortunate that most job aspirants do not pay sufficient attention to writing a good application to a prospective employer. They feel that all that the employer is interested in is their academic achievements. This is not true. The prospective employer is really interested in knowing how well a prospective employee can help him achieve what he

expects through the job. The person who can convince him of this gets the job. It is as simple as that.

An application for a job is a personal representation of the prospective employee. When the application reaches the prospective employer, he forms an impression immediately. The application can, therefore, make or mar the prospects of getting the job. It deserves special attention. Let us discuss all the aspects of this important step towards a super job.

Applying for the Job

When you come across a job opportunity that you feel is just the right one for you, it is time to write to your prospective employer. Since there can be many applications for some jobs, the employers might desire that it should be made in a prescribed format or on a prescribed form that they supply on request, or on payment. Sometimes the forms can also be downloaded from the website. If the application is not required on a specific format, it is absolutely in order to apply on a plain white sheet of paper, neatly typewritten or handwritten. If you have a personal letterhead, you can use it for the purpose. An application should neither look fancy or ostentatious nor should it be on business letterheads or fancy paper used to convey greetings.

When you sit down to draft your application for the job, always remember one thing: the prospective employer, like all other employers, desires to hire a person who can help him to further his own personal interests. His interest in the job is limited to what he can get out of it. Your interest in the job is secondary to him. If the employer makes an effort to keep the employees satisfied, it is only because by doing so he can only fulfill his personal interests better. Your immediate interest is that of securing the job. This can be achieved only when you convince him that he would benefit from giving you employment. This makes it necessary that your application must convince him that you are the right person to help him fulfill what he desires.

When your application is in response to an advertisement, there will be many aspirants for the job. It would not be possible for the employer to meet all the prospective employees, and therefore it is customary to shortlist the applicants by scrutinizing the applications. An important purpose that the application must fulfill is that it must convey that you are worthy of being called for an interview. Therefore, the application must convincingly convey your qualifications, abilities and skills with particular reference to what the job entails.

While preparing the draft of the application, be honest about what you have to convey. Do not write anything that you know is incorrect or false. Employers have a way of finding the truth.. You can fool some people sometimes, but you cannot get away with it. This can put you in an awkward position later.

Writing the Application

When the application is desired on a prescribed application form, the immediate care that is necessary is that every column must be filled. Do not leave any line or box incomplete. If some information is not available, write the reason for the same. For example, when you make an application, the results of the final year exams may not have been declared. It is also possible that the results might have been declared but the mark sheet may not have been received. In such a situation you can write: "Result awaited" or "Mark sheet not received".

Another reason that the form must be completely filled is that many employers may like to tabulate the applications on the computer, and each column is entered in the computer directly from the form. With some columns blank the tabulation becomes difficult. In the event of any problem, it is the applicant who will suffer by being eliminated from the list. To a prospective employer, all applications are only a path to the person he desires to employ. If one application is incomplete, he will move on to the next applicant.

Some forms downloaded from a website can be filled on the computer and also submitted online. When this is not possible, the forms should be filled on a typewriter. If one does not have access to a typewriter, the form can be filled by hand preferably in capital letters, or in legible handwriting. Do not strike off or over-write on a word. The reader should not have any difficulty in reading any entry.

When it is necessary to paste a photograph on the form, one must ensure that it is a good passport size photograph with the person looking directly at the photographer. The photograph must be securely pasted. It would be useful to write one's name and identification at the back of the photograph before pasting so that if due to any reason it comes off, the photograph and the application form can be reasonably identified.

When an application is not to be submitted on a prescribed form but is to be submitted in the normal course, there are three distinct parts that need the attention of the applicant. The first part pertains to the abilities and skills of the person as related to the job, the second part refers to the documents that need to be annexed in proof of the first part, and finally there is the covering letter that contains the request to be considered for the job. Let us consider each part one by one.

Think it over...

Man's main task in life is to give birth to himself, to become what he potentially is. The most important product of his effort is his own personality.

— *Erich Fromm*

Curriculum Vitae

Curriculum vitae, or CV as it is popularly called, is a brief account of a person's qualifications and previous occupations sent with a job application. It is also known as a résumé, meaning a summary of one's abilities and achievements. Another related word is bio-data, where *bio* means having to do with living beings, and *data* refers to facts or statistics. Together, bio-data means facts or details about a person. In different places and situations, one of the three words is used. While the first two are generally used when applying for jobs, the third one is used when introducing a person to a group or gathering, as in a formal function.

At the outset, writing a curriculum vitae or résumé appears to be an easy task, particularly when one is writing about oneself, but in reality it is not as simple as one would think it to be. Unfortunately, many capable persons fail to be called for an interview simply because they failed to present a convincing CV or résumé. What is worse is that most people fail to recognize that not being invited for an interview is not because of lack of abilities and skills, or because of a negative or partisan attitude of the prospective employer, but for the simple reason of a poorly drafted CV or résumé. Here are a few time-tested ideas for writing a CV that creates a positive impact with the prospective employer.

- **Remember the purpose**. The purpose of sending a CV or résumé to a prospective employer is not to get the job but rather to convince him that the applicant possesses the necessary abilities and skills, and deserves to be invited for the interview. A good CV or résumé puts the candidate a little ahead of others.

- **Begin with your name**. Some people have long names that in some cultures include the father's name and also the village or town from where the family hails. That makes the name lengthy and unwieldy. Use the name you are generally known by. Most people have a first name, which is the popular name one is known by amongst friends and relatives, and a surname, which is the family name shared by everyone. In some cultures, the middle name is the father's name and is used in abbreviated form as an initial. For example, James Peter Anderson would be known as James P. Anderson, or even as Jim Anderson. Write the name you like to be known by.

- **Give the complete address**. The prospective employer must know at what address to contact you for calling you for an interview. Unfortunately, many educated people do not put the address information in the correct order. The name on the top must be followed by the house or building name, if any, the floor, if it is a large multi-storeyed building, the house number, the name of the street, the name of the locality and the name of the town with its postal code. In international mail, the name of the country must also be mentioned boldly.

If this were the first job, one would obviously have one address where one is living. However, in some cases when one is working or living elsewhere, as in a college or university hostel, one would have another address which is obviously only a temporary address. In such a situation, it may be necessary to mention both addresses. First, the permanent address, which is the home address, and second, the temporary address for immediate contact.

- **Give the telephone numbers**. In the present age when everyone is in a hurry, many prospective employers get in touch with the applicants on the telephone. Do mention the city code and the telephone number/s. If it is not your number, you can mention that a message could be left at that number and you would respond back. It could be your father's number or that of your neighbour. The mobile number could follow the landline number/s. Many school and college students have personal mobile numbers.

- **The email address**. Except for the elder generation who were not exposed to computers, most people own and use computers every day. Those who do not own laptops or desktops use cyber cafes to access information. An email ID makes it convenient to reach out and also be quickly reached through the Internet.

Use a dignified email address for job searches and professional use.

- **Age, marital status and family status**. In some countries, this information is considered necessary and must be mentioned. However, in some countries, as in the U.S.A., this information is not provided. To mention the age, one could give it by mentioning the date of birth. In all government jobs, this is necessary because retirement depends upon it. Marital status and family status may be important to some prospective employers, but many may not bother about it.

- **Stating one's objective**. Many aspiring employees include an objective as a part of the CV. One may write something like: "It is my objective to give of my best in service." Most employers would not bother about such objectives. Unless an objective improves the CV or is of interest to the position you are applying for, it may not be advisable to include such a statement in the CV.

- **List all your accomplishments**. This is the part that would interest the prospective employer the most. It is this part of the CV that describes your abilities, skills and accomplishments. The employer analyses this information to gauge your potential as an employee.

  To begin with, make a list of all your accomplishments. These will obviously include your achievements at school and college, skills that you have acquired, personal projects you may have been involved with, awards that you may have received, the jobs you may have undertaken and special achievements that you might have gained. The list may appear impressive to some and not so to others. Your accomplishments are proof of the effort you have made and the success that you have attained. Once this list is ready, it is time to sort and organize it for easy comprehension. The presentation will need to be consistent with the kind of position you are applying for. The list can generally be itemized under different heads as described hereafter:

(a) **Academic accomplishments**. All employers are interested in an employee's academic qualifications and accomplishments. This is particularly important if this is the first job you are applying for. Begin with the most recent achievements and go backwards to your high school record. For example, if you were applying for a teaching position, you will need to have completed a degree in Education, followed by say MA in English, Bachelor (Honours) degree with subjects, and school education at +2 level and class 10 level. Mention percentages and positions, if any. Some educational institutions and universities are held in special respect for the kind of education they impart. If so, mention the details. They add weight to your CV because of the educational culture these institutions are known for.

(b) **Jobs and positions held**. Certain jobs and positions require work experience and the employer would like to know and analyse the same for every applicant. List the position held, responsibilities involved, special accomplishments, if any, the period of employment and the name of the employer. In analysing the information, every prospective employer is interested in the applicant's skills and accomplishments and not in the responsibilities entrusted to the person. The achievements need to be emphasized.

While the details of the jobs and positions held are appreciated for middle level and senior level positions, most employers look at these with some suspicion for junior level positions. The principle reason for this is that those who change jobs too often, as reflected in the CV, project the image that they could be unstable or opportunistic and may not be good long-term employees. Young aspirants need to be careful about this, and they will certainly be questioned about it if invited for an interview.

(c) **Experience in voluntary activities**. Let us not overlook that work experience in voluntary activities is just as useful as in a job. Therefore, if one has such experience, it should be mentioned in the CV. For example, if a person organised a successful conference for a youth organisation during college days, it would be evidence of the organisational ability of the person. There could have been many occasions for doing social work; activities which are encouraged at both school and college level. Many young people use these skills in their social life in a voluntary capacity and gain much experience in return. This experience can be useful at the workplace.

(d) **Special skills**. Good communication skills are important in all aspects of life including the workplace. Many employers do not mention this in an advertisement for a job, nonetheless, they are very important. If a person has excelled at debating in school or college or was involved in editing the college magazine, it would be worthwhile to mention this in the CV. These qualities provide evidence of good communication skills, which can be very useful at the workplace.

(e) **Awards at all levels**. Young people start getting awards and recognitions at the school level for academics, games and sports, public speaking and for leadership qualities. These are evidence of special abilities and skills. All prospective employers look for such information in a CV. These skills can be used in offices and project a multifaceted personality that can be developed usefully.

Think it over...

Personality projection is like any other investment. The thing goes on.

— Lloyd C. Douglas

Blowing Your Own Trumpet

The purpose of the CV should be to be invited to the interview. It should provide ample information to arouse the interest of the prospective employer. This involves writing about one's abilities and accomplishments; the CV should make it evident that the applicant is a young aspiring employee ready to deliver. The CV should reflect the confidence of the applicant. However, we cannot overlook that over-confidence leads to pride and thereafter to arrogance. A fine line divides the two. Confidence is appreciated, not arrogance. One cannot afford to cross this line. While on one hand, it is necessary to highlight one's accomplishments, on the other hand, it is essential that one does not cross the fine line to be labeled proud or arrogant.

How should one describe personal accomplishments? Here is a list of common words that are descriptive and are most frequently used: acquired, adapted, administered, analysed, assembled, assisted, audited, calculated, changed, collaborated, composed, conducted, constructed, contracted, coordinated, created, demonstrated, designed, developed, devised, discovered, drafted, edited, eliminated, enforced, established, evaluated, expanded, forecasted, formed, founded, generated, guided, hired, implemented, improved, informed, interpreted, interviewed, launched, maintained, managed, marketed, minimized, motivated, negotiated, obtained, operated, organised, oversaw, performed, planned, prevented, produced, promoted, provided, publicized, published, recruited, reorganized, reported, researched, resolved, reviewed, selected, set up, simplified, solved, surveyed, staffed, supervised, taught, tested, trained, utilised.

Use these words to describe your achievements. The description of your accomplishments should highlight your strengths. The use of the words makes it easier to frame sentences. Yet it is necessary that this must be done discreetly. Do not over-exaggerate or write what is not true. The secret lies in putting in an extra effort to draft one's accomplishments without sounding offensive or arrogant. The time spent on this exercise would be useful because you are describing accomplishments till a particular time, and you would only add on with time and experience.

Additional Information

We have already discussed that experience and accomplishments attained in voluntary projects should be included in the CV. They highlight a person's abilities and skills. New aspirants often ask: "What about hobbies? Should they be mentioned in the CV? What about achievements in the games field? How do prospective employers look at that? Would an employer accept them as an individual's strengths?"

It is natural to seek answers to these questions. The truth is that employers are human beings and like everyone else have their likes and dislikes. An employer would be clear what he expects to be done, and looks for abilities and skills that contribute to success in the area of work he has to offer. His immediate need is precisely to look for these abilities and skills in the applicants. If additional skills are available, as can be confirmed from the additional information provided, that adds weight in favour of one candidate against another.

People have a variety of hobbies, as varied as collecting stamps to reading or watching football on the TV. Some hobbies such as painting, photography and writing articles or short stories are creative. Some of these could be useful at the workplace. Voluntary activities too have their pluses and minuses. While some of these are looked at with favour, there are others that are disfavoured because of reasons like political leanings and attachments, or even religious beliefs that a prospective employer may not approve.

In including additional information, the applicant should answer a simple question. Will the additional information convey that I am better equipped for a particular job than one who is not so equipped? If the answer is "yes", then include it in the CV otherwise don't. Leave it for a later time like the interview when you would definitely know what the employer desires.

Tailoring the CV

Most aspiring young job seekers prepare a CV or résumé and feel that this can be used as a standard CV to be sent to all prospective employers. This is not the right thing to do. One must appreciate that no two employers are the same, and neither are their needs. Each CV must be tailor-made for a particular job. This means that before you apply for a job you must get as much information about the company, its owners, products, policies and other similar information as is possible. Once you have this information, you can relate your accomplishments to the company's requirements. This would also be useful when you are invited for the interview.

Tailoring a CV does not mean that you need to rewrite the CV every time you apply for a job, but only to make certain additions and deletions in certain parts of the CV to make it appear custom-made. Sending a readymade CV to all prospective employers is like throwing bait into the river and waiting to see if a fish would bite. The prospective employer immediately figures it out that he is one in the many and does not give it the attention that every job seeker desires to receive. A tailor-made CV has better chances of getting an interview letter.

Think it over...

We seek to cover truth by the creatures of our imagination and endeavour to escape from reality to a world of dreams.

— *Jawaharlal Nehru*

Putting the CV Together

When all the information has been collected, it is time to put the CV together as a document for the prospective employer. Have you observed why some books are easier to read and understand than others? These books are written in simple language and move from one subject to another step by step. Besides, the publisher ensures that the fonts used are readable, large and attractive. In the same way, the CV needs to be presented in an attractive format, well typed, preferably on a computer. Here are a few guidelines for getting the CV ready.

- **The type of font used**. Select a font that is easy to read. Arial is a popular font used by MS Office users. Some prefer Times New Roman, Bookman or Courier. Whatever font you use, ensure that it is simple and readable, and not fancy like the fonts used in greeting cards. Some people make the mistake of using too many different kinds of fonts. For a document like a CV, it is best to use a single font. If you want to use more, do not exceed two or three different types. Ensure that they match well with each other.

- **Size of the font**. The size of the font is important to make the CV easy to read. It is suggested that the size of the font should be 10 to 14 points; a popular size is 12 points. If the CV is short, as in the case of new aspiring job seekers, use the larger font size. While the CV could be in 12 points, some details like accomplishments could be in 10 points to accommodate more matter in a limited space.

- **The length of the CV**. It is suggested that the CV should be in two typed pages. If the entire details cannot be included within two pages, one could carry over to the third page. The longer versions are for middle and senior level positions from an applicant who desires to give details of accomplishments and experience at lower levels.

- **Editing the CV**. Very few people possess editing skills. Here are a few hints to present a neat readable CV.

  (a) **Present details logically**. Categorize the information and present them under different sub-headings like personal details, educational achievements, working experience, social interests and other details.

  (b) **Spellings and grammar**. Wrong spellings and grammatical errors project an image of carelessness. These must be checked. To avoid grammatical errors, write simple sentences. Use words that are easy to understand.

  (c) **Cut out the unnecessary frills**. After the initial draft of the CV is ready, put it aside for two days. Read it again, deleting words and sentences that appear superfluous. Cutting out the frills makes the matter crisp and readable.

(d) **Spread the matter uniformly**. The written matter should be well spread out. When the matter overflows from one page to another, ensure that the page is at least half full. If it is not possible, cut out portions to accommodate the matter without having to write a few lines on the next page. This can also be achieved by adjusting the font size. However, the readability should not be compromised at any cost.

Typing the CV

The CV should be printed on plain white good quality paper in A4 size. Do not use fancy stationery. Do not print in colour or use designs unless you are applying for a job in a designing establishment where such applications could be acceptable. Leave a fair margin on all sides. A margin of 1½ inch on the left side and one inch on the other three sides creates a fair balance. Both inkjet and laser printers do a neat job.

Supporting Documents

It is customary to attach copies of certificates, mark sheets and references to support the information about your qualifications and accomplishments. Do not send any originals. They can be shown at the time of the interview. When a prospective employer desires references, you could draw upon your good relations with your family doctor, your father's friends, or even the parents of your friends. Those with work experience can give references from their past employers. While supporting documents give credibility to the information provided in the CV, it has been observed that most job aspirants overdo this by enclosing as many as 5 or more references and a dozen certificates about proficiency in games and proof of participation in debates or competitions during school days. These only add to the bulk and serve no purpose. The prospective employer is interested in your abilities and skills relevant to the job he desires to be done. Do not send documents that are not relevant to the job.

A Photograph

Job aspirants often ask if a photograph should be a part of the application for a job. Some employers specifically ask that a photograph should be attached with the application. In many countries like Germany, a photograph must be attached with the application, whereas in countries like U.S.A. and Canada, the employers disqualify candidates who send photographs. It is, therefore, necessary to understand what is customary in a particular culture, and also what the employer desires. When in doubt, do not send it. You could write in the covering letter that a photograph could be sent, if desired.

Think it over...

Letters have their power of speech, which tongues do not possess.

— *Rabindra Nath Tagore*

The Covering Letter

The CV would be a complete document, describing the details and accomplishments of the applicant and supported by attached documents. It would not be addressed to any specific person or organisation, as it could be used for applying to several jobs. Therefore, it is necessary to write a covering letter that explains the purpose of the accompanying CV and supporting documents.

The covering letter should make it clear who is writing it, for whom it is meant and what is its purpose. The letter should be as brief as possible and need not repeat the information that is already included in the CV and supported by the enclosures. It must be restricted to a page, must mention the position and the job applied for, and must include a request that the job may be given to the applicant. The letter must be neatly typed on white A4 size paper and should be a good representative of the person who is writing it.

Things to Remember

Here are a few things that you will do well to remember:

- Follow instructions, if any, in the job advertisement.
- Put in your best efforts to write the CV.
- The CV must highlight your strengths and accomplishments.
- Be as brief as possible. Give the maximum information in the least number of words.
- Revise the CV as often as is possible.
- Check the application before enclosing it in the envelope.

Things to Avoid

Here are a few things you will do well to avoid:

- Don't be shy to write about your accomplishments.
- Don't include irrelevant information about yourself or the family.
- Don't use your current employer's address, email or phone numbers.
- Don't over-qualify yourself for the job.
- Don't attach unnecessary documents like a birth certificate, copies of diplomas, etc. with the application.
- Don't lie about anything.

The Envelope

Assemble the covering letter, the CV and the supporting enclosures by pinning them together or tying them together at the top left-hand corner. The documents should not have more than two folds to be accommodated in a business size envelope. This is possible only if there are four or five sheets. If they are in excess of this number, fold them halfway and dispatch them in a larger envelope.

The envelope must be properly addressed and must also have the sender's address. If the prospective employer has specifically mentioned it, do not overlook to mark the envelope with special remarks like "For Management Trainees", "Junior Executives", "Jobs Advertisement no: xx" so that on arrival the envelope is forwarded to the appropriate department without delay. Send the envelope through registered post or Speed Post.

Copy of the Application

Most job aspirants feel that they remember whatever they have written and do not keep a copy of their job application. This is wrong. It is necessary that one must keep a copy of every job application that one sends. We discussed it earlier that the CV must be tailor-made for every job application. The covering letter too would be different. That makes it necessary that the copy of the revised CV and covering letter must be on record. The postal receipt should be pasted on the covering letter for reference. It can be very embarrassing when the prospective employer makes an enquiry about the application and the applicant does not have a copy to check with.

Points to Ponder...

- It is necessary that to get a job one must get in touch with prospective employers.
- The job application should convey the message that you have the skills and abilities to fulfill the employer's needs.
- The job application should be a fair representative of the job seeker.
- The curriculum vitae or résumé should highlight the job seeker's skills, abilities and achievements.
- One must put in the best efforts to draft the curriculum vitae or résumé.

- The details in the curriculum vitae or résumé should project the job seeker's confidence but should not cross the line to project pride or arrogance.
- Documents to confirm one's achievements must be attached to the CV.
- The CV must be tailored to be consistent with the job requirements.
- The CV must be put together methodically, using the best of modern facilities.
- The application document must not be big and unwieldy.
- A photograph must be pasted on the CV, if required.
- The job application should be in the form of a letter to which the CV and other documents are attached.
- Revise and check up on every detail before putting the application into the envelope, which must be of an appropriate size and neatly addressed.
- Always keep a copy of the documents sent to the prospective employer.

The Interview

On receiving an application for a job, the prospective employer browses through it. If it comes close to what he has in mind, it is put aside for further action. If it does not, it is rejected. Some prospective employers inform the applicants that they do not fit into the kind of work they have in mind. A majority does not respond back. A few place the applications in a file for future consideration, if desired.

If an applicant does not hear from a prospective employer within a reasonable period of time, one can presume that he or she is not being called for the interview. This is frustrating to a lot of new aspirants for a job. This is the way of the world, and this must be accepted as a part of life. One should not lose confidence in oneself, or in the system. There could be several reasons for not being called for the interview. There may be too many candidates for the same job. There may be candidates better qualified than you. It is also likely that the job may have been filled through a promotion within the organisation.

Applying for a job is very much like a new author submitting his manuscript for publication. Every author, however popular he or she may be, has received his or her share of rejection slips. Many proudly claim they have enough to line the wall of their room. It is very disheartening in the beginning, but soon one gets used to them. In every field, everyone has had his or her share of rejected applications.

One should not lose confidence. To succeed, one must persist. The secret lies in keep trying until one is invited for an interview. Then you are face to face with the prospective employer. Your success lies in convincing him of your abilities and skills. This is possible only through preparation.

Preparing for the Interview

When an application fulfills the basic requirements as advertised and desired by the prospective employer, the applicant will get an interview call. It is a simple courtesy to acknowledge an interview call when you receive it. Confirm the place, day and time mentioned in the letter.

To succeed in an interview, one must be well prepared. The chances are that the period from the day you get the call letter and the interview may be short. When one is eager to get the job, one should not wait for the interview letter to begin preparing for the interview. One must find out as much as one can about the prospective employer and the job. The basic purpose of the interview is to assess the personality and the capabilities of the applicants, and how the prospective employer can use them to promote his personal interests through the job that was advertised.

Find out all that you can about your prospective employer's company–its set-up, branches, products and services. If possible, one would do well to find out about the responsibilities and the privileges of the position one has applied for. Such information can be collected from the advertisements in the national press, house journals, the local distributors, and even the local retailers. It would also be useful to collect information about other companies in the same trade. With this information, one will have a wider perspective to appreciate the prospective employer's needs and understand and answer important questions at the interview. Some interviewers may look at the situation from a different angle. Therefore, if the interviewer is not inclined to ask such questions, do not try to impress him with your knowledge.

One would do well to have a file containing a copy of the CV and the original documents in support of the achievements mentioned in the application ready. If you are already working, you may need to apply for leave to be present at the interview. Employers understand that young people are ambitious and desire better positions, yet they are never happy about their workers leaving them. Therefore, when you ask for leave, unless it is specifically desired that you have a clearance certificate from your present employer, it is sufficient to mention in your leave application that you require it to attend to personal matters.

The Purpose of the Interview

The hiring of new personnel by a prospective employer becomes necessary because of a definite need, and it is on the basis of this need that he searches for appropriate persons who can fulfill it. The purpose of the interview is to provide the prospective employer an opportunity to assess the personality and capabilities of the candidates who have applied for the job. He assesses them in relation to the purpose he has in his mind. An employer hires workers directly or indirectly to help him provide a product or service which benefits him. He appreciates that an employee is not a machine that can be installed and expected to give the desired performance under given circumstances. Since the human factor is very important, it is imperative for the employer to assess the individual's personality, knowledge, performance and efficiency, and also how he can use these to his personal advantage.

The prospective employer critically assesses the image that different applicants project at the interview. The interview provides a fair opportunity to do this. Employers are particularly interested in the general health of the individual, the personality as projected by one's body language, manners, and the way one dresses. The interview also provides an opportunity to the employer to confirm the facts mentioned in the application and the CV. He would also like to assess the general knowledge, special interests and achievements, the ability to learn new skills, and the attitude towards the job being offered. The ability to take decisions is vital to many jobs. He would like to assess the candidate's ability in this field also. The interview also provides an opportunity to talk about one's past successes and failures, and how the candidate may have reacted to them. The applicant's reactions and answers to the interviewer's questions help him conclude how a particular candidate can possibly help him achieve his purpose through the job.

Think it over...

The truth about man is simple and universal and does not change with time and place.

— *J. Krishnamurthi*

Interview Essentials

The interview is a very important link between the candidate and the job. To attain success, one must understand every aspect of the interview. Every prospective candidate will do well to understand the following points:

- **Reach in time**. One must reach the place of the interview punctually at the appointed time, or rather a little before time. One must allow for delays because of traffic and other factors.

- **Be appropriately dressed**. Your sense of dress tells a lot about your personality and your attitude towards the job. The dress should be neither too formal nor too casual. Wear a day suit, or if the weather and the circumstances do not permit it, a white shirt with a necktie and a coloured trouser will be all right. Wear either brown or black shoes to match the trouser. Avoid fancy footwear. Ensure that you have had a shave, have clean nails, and the hair is properly groomed. The lady candidates too need to dress modestly, avoiding heavy makeup and jewellery.

- **Carry the documents in a neat file**. Do not tuck them in an ugly envelope, or stuff them in the pocket. It is unfortunate to have candidates put up crushed documents. When copies need to be submitted, ensure that they are neat and legible. Dull and illegible copies create a bad impression.

- **Report your arrival**. When you arrive at the venue for the interview, report your arrival to the person concerned. This will give you an opportunity for an early interview.

- **Assess the situation**. When directed to be seated and wait for the interview, look around to assess the situation. What kind of an impression do you get about the premises? What do you think about the staff behaviour? How many candidates are in the fray for the job? What is your impression about the candidates? The answers provide useful information.

- **Observe self-control**. Do not try to become friendly with the receptionist or with the other candidates. If you get into conversation, talk about general things. Do not start comparing notes and qualifications with other candidates. They are your competitors. They seek the same position as you do.

- **Remain calm**. Avoid unnecessary tension. If you are anxious, take a few deep breaths. Relax. Say a prayer. It helps calm the nerves.

- **Do not smoke**. Many organisations prohibit smoking on the premises. Even if you see some of the interviewers smoking, avoid it altogether.

- **Do not chew gum or eat anything**. Even if you have not had breakfast and are hungry wait until the interview is over. If the mouth feels dry, have a glass of water.

- **Read to keep busy**. You can read the newspaper or a book until you are called for the interview. If you prefer to read a book, avoid cheap fiction. The prospective employer may have read it too, but when it comes to employees, most employers desire that their employees should read constructive and useful books.

The Interview

In an interview the first impression is very important. When you are called for the interview, remember to put your best foot forward. Take a deep breath and enter with a smile. This helps in getting over the initial nervousness. Take a quick look around the room and greet the interviewer/s with a smile.

Sit down only when asked to. Place the file before you. Here are a few ideas on creating the correct impression on the interviewers:

- **Breaking the ice**. Let the interviewer take the initiative. Let him or her start the conversation.

- **Be well prepared**. Read your CV before going for an interview. Most experienced interviewers begin by asking questions to which they already know the answers because they are on the CV. This is to put the candidate at ease and build a rapport to understand the candidate better.

- **Self-introduction**. Many interviewers ask the candidates to tell something about them. When a candidate has not thought about this, one is at a loss for appropriate words. This could put the interview off track. Be ready to talk about yourself, highlighting your strengths and achievements. Do mention your weaknesses along with the efforts you are making to overcome them.

- **Be prepared for embarrassing questions**. The interviewers are as eager to know about your weaknesses as they are about your strengths. It is natural for everyone to have both strengths and weaknesses. Do not let it embarrass you. The interviewer does not wish to criticize or embarrass you, but he wants to know if you are aware about your weaknesses and what you are doing to overcome them over a period.

- **Be modest about your achievements**. The interviewer would like to observe how you react to your achievements. Some candidates are over-enthusiastic about them and go to great lengths to explain. Do not give too many details unless specifically asked. Time is a crucial factor for the interviewer. Be brief and to the point.

- **Highlight your skills and abilities**. The interviewer would like to assess your skills and abilities as highlighted in the CV. He is bound to ask pertinent questions to gain information about your skills. He will want to hear you rather than speak himself. Do not interrupt him when he is speaking. Hear the questions or remarks carefully, and respond appropriately, speaking clearly and audibly. For a good rapport, look straight at the interviewer.

- **Do not let an interview panel make you anxious**. Sometimes there may be more than one interviewer. They may ask questions that are far apart. To seek time, you could tactfully repeat the question to confirm if you have understood the question correctly. Answer questions in as simple a language as you can manage. Good conversation skills are useful.

- **Speak straight and simple**. Do not pretend to be knowledgeable and use high flung words in your conversation. Use simple words used in everyday conversation. Never use slang or foul words.

- **No smoking please**. Some interviewers smoke and, as a matter of courtesy, may offer you a cigarette. Even if you smoke, refuse the offer courteously. He will not insist about it.

- **Special interests**. The interviewer is bound to touch upon your special interests if they are mentioned in the CV. He would want to know how they influence your hopes and aspirations. Do not give undue importance unless they are connected with skills necessary for the job. The interviewer is interested in how you can fulfill his needs through the job, and not how you benefit from them.

- **Family circumstances**. The interviewer could sometimes ask you questions pertaining to your family. You are free to refuse certain details that you feel infringe your privacy. The interviewer's interest would be limited to how your family circumstances could affect job responsibilities, as one would need to keep away from home on outstation selling assignments. In the same way, little children could prevent a mother from full-time job responsibilities.

- **General knowledge questions**. The interviewer could encourage you to express your opinion about a current problem. Do not take advantage of the situation to discuss personal philosophies or show that you are learned or clever. Keep your opinion brief, clear and to the point. Your power of expression is at test. Keep the limited time in mind. The interviewer will appreciate it.

- **Provocative questions**. Sometimes the interviewer could test your reactions in special circumstances. He could ask you provocative questions, or broach controversial subjects. Such situations demand great tact and patience. Do not be provoked under any circumstances. Display complete cool, and discuss your viewpoint with a smile.

- **Questions to which you have no answers**. It is possible that the interviewer may ask you something you do not know anything about. Do not hesitate to admit your ignorance. One cannot be expected to know everything. If it is something vital you should have known or been aware about, you can still admit your ignorance and apologize for it. Your frankness will be appreciated.

- **An eye for shortcomings**. All interviewers have an eye for discrepancies. They will positively ask you questions pertaining to past failures and shortcomings, if any. When faced with such a situation, do not try to fool the interviewer. Explain your viewpoint reasonably. The interviewer would not be interested in why you failed, but what you learnt from your failure.

- **Changing jobs**. If you were changing jobs, the interviewer would like to know what has necessitated the change. Explain the situation reasonably. Do not be critical of those with whom you work presently or have worked in the past. It would be more acceptable if you were to say that the circumstances did not suit you, rather than that your present or past employers had made things difficult for you.

- **Interviewers' whims and fancies**. All interviewers are like ordinary people and may be guided by their own whims and fancies. We cannot overlook that despite their views they have an eye for people with ability. Do not contradict their views. You may not agree with them but do confess that you have learnt about another viewpoint on the subject.

- **Clearing doubts**. The interviewers may not immediately disclose whether you have been selected or not, but before concluding the interview they may inquire if you would like to ask them anything in particular. You can avail yourself of this opportunity to clarify doubts, if any, about the prospects of the job, the fringe benefits, etc. Be brief and specific.

- **Leave with a word of gratitude**. Interviewers are busy people. Thank them for providing you an opportunity to talk to them. Do not leave behind an impression that you have encroached upon their time.

Think it over...

The study of man in society cannot become an exact science. Man is the future of man.

— *Dr. S. Radhakrisnan*

Answering Questions Convincingly

Behaving like a majority of students who fail to answer exam questions, complaining that the examiner had included questions from outside the syllabus, most candidates blame the interviewer for their own failings. In an interview, there are no tough questions. There are only questions that one is not prepared for at that moment of time. To avoid such a situation, here are a few hints that would be useful:

- **Be prepared**. Every situation is different. To be successful, one must be prepared for it. Stop being complacent. Prepare!

- **Know yourself well**. Be ready with a self-introduction that includes details of your education, skills, achievements and experience. Be prepared to talk about your strengths and weaknesses and what lessons you have gained?

- **Know the prospective employer**. Know what he desires from the job he has offered. Know all that you can about him.

- **Prepare a list of possible questions**. Many questions asked at interviews are common. Many are special too. Figure out what special questions you could be asked. This will give you an opportunity to think about the job and prepare for the interview.

- **Check your CV**. Many questions arise from the information provided by you in your CV. Review the facts given in it. What possible questions can the interviewer ask on the basis of the information? Be prepared to answer them.

- **Develop a wider outlook towards life**. Too many people look at life from a narrow point of view. This does not give them the whole picture. Look at the past and the future. Look at the current situation. How do the past and the future influence it? Learn to control your thoughts and be prepared to take a complete look at life.

- **Appreciate the positive and ignore the negative**. Take a positive outlook of individuals, organisations and situations. While a positive attitude strengthens your beliefs and abilities, a negative outlook saps you of your energy and makes you tense.

- **Be honest**. Answering convincingly does not mean passing something false as true. It means accepting the reality that everyone has strengths and weaknesses simultaneously. Being honest means telling others how you are tackling the habit of procrastination by learning the art of prioritization.

- **Be humble**. A consistent achiever convinces others through activities and not through words. Humility is the hallmark of great achievers. Do not let pride or arrogance colour your speech.

- **Use simple words and sentences**. Everyone appreciates simplicity in word and action. When answering questions, use simple words. Use common everyday vocabulary everyone understands. You will be appreciated for it.

Changing Jobs Related Questions

All employers desire that their employees should continue to work with them. It saves them from the problems of searching for new employees, training them to fit their organisation and making them productive. However, all employers also understand that every employee has a family to support, a career to grow with and seeks to grow in position with time and experience. Some organisations can provide this growth while others cannot. Most employers understand this problem, yet they are always suspicious about candidates who are already working and desire to move in as a part of personal growth. This is bound to evoke several questions during the interview and the candidate must be ready to answer them. Here are a few useful guidelines:

- **Be well prepared**. Every situation is bound to be different and so will the questions be. Make a list of possible questions that the interviewer could ask you.

Think of good convincing answers. When you have given sufficient thought to the problem, you would have valid answers.

- **Be honest**. Do not misguide the interviewer about your intentions. In all likelihood, he would be more experienced and knowledgeable than you. Explain that the change is a part of your career growth, or that it brings you closer to your family and other concerns.

- **Do not let down past employers**. This is a common fault with many job aspirants. They will speak badly about their past bosses and the organisations they have worked for. If this is your attitude about the past relationships, there are bleak chances of building new alliances.

- **Highlight your career goals**. All employers appreciate employees who wish to grow in their jobs. When you explain your career goals, it becomes easier to relate them to change in jobs.

Think it over...

Every man has three characters–that which he exhibits, that which he has, and that which he thinks he has.

— *Alphonse Karr*

Group Interview

Sometimes, particularly when the number of candidates invited for the interview is large, or when the interviewers are especially interested in observing candidates for initiative and leadership qualities, a group interview may be conducted prior to a one-to-one interview. The group interview may involve small groups of 4 to 6 candidates or the whole lot seated together with the interviewer initiating and controlling the discussion on a subject of his choice.

The problem with a group interview is that one does not know what to expect. It will entirely depend upon what the prospective employer feels about his needs. The challenge before every candidate is to stand out above the others. This requires one to possess good leadership qualities and also good communication skills. Here are some common observations to create a good impression in a group interview:

- **Be well informed about the company**. Unless you can get to know all about the company you want to work for, you will not be able to speak from the viewpoint the prospective employer desires. Search for information on the Internet, through dealers, finance companies and customers who use the company's products and services.

- **Occupy a seat with an advantage**. All the seats are not the same. Sit where you can be seen and heard. In a roundtable arrangement some are at a disadvantage. Be in direct view of the interviewer and others.

- **Introduce yourself**. The interviewer will normally ask everyone to introduce oneself before the start of the discussion. If so, pronounce your name clearly and audibly. If this procedure is not followed, announce your name before you speak.

- **Prepare a brief introduction**. You may be asked to introduce yourself briefly. Do not leave it to the last minute. Prepare a brief introduction that summarizes your education, skills, career goals and experience. Practice giving this introduction at home.

- **Listen carefully**. Understand the purpose of the group discussion as explained by the interviewer. If you have not understood any point, do not hesitate to ask the interviewer to clarify it for everyone's benefit. Even when others speak, listen attentively. Note down important concepts that you agree or disagree with. This will give you an opportunity to show that there can be many views about the same thing.
- **Speak confidently**. When invited to speak, stand confidently looking directly at the interviewer or the audience, as the situation requires. Choose words carefully. Place the correct emphasis on important words.
- **Always be courteous**. You may need to disagree with certain opinions expressed deliberately by the interviewer or others. Do so courteously. It is all right to disagree, but wrong to be disagreeable. Courtesy is always appreciated.
- **Act like a leader**. A popular purpose of group interviews is to look for leadership skills. Do not speak loudly or aggressively to highlight the leader in you. A good leader is confident, possesses good listening skills, speaks assertively (not aggressively) and is in general a facilitator. He or she seeks everyone's co-operation and carries others along. Praise others for good ideas. Highlight what is good for everyone.
- **Accept criticism happily**. Just as you may praise good ideas expressed by others, a few may criticize you to express their own superiority. Do not let this discourage you or put you off. Take criticism and praise in the same stride. They are two sides of the same coin.

- **Remain calm and cool**. It is common for people to use provocative language in any kind of discussion. Some of the remarks may hit you directly. Do not let this provoke you. Your purpose is not to show the other person down, but rather to express your own superior handling of a situation.

- **Keep smiling**. It is not easy to keep smiling all the time particularly when a person may be under stress of a group interview. However, it is the smiling person everyone likes to work with. Therefore, if you want to succeed, keep smiling. You will be well compensated for your effort.

- **End with a word of gratitude**. At the close of the interview, thank the interviewer and others for making the discussion useful.

Think it over...

We can hardly realize now the blissful quietitude of the pre-telephone epoch.

— *Norman Douglas*

Telephone Interview

When there are a large number of job aspirants and some are from other towns, some employers find it useful to have a telephone interview that may last for 15 to 30 minutes to get additional inputs before inviting a candidate to visit the office for a final face to face interview. This saves a lot of time for the employer and the candidates. These interviews are like any other interviews except that the candidate is not sitting before an interview panel. One or more persons may conduct the phone interview. Here are a few hints that would be helpful to have a successful interview:

- **Take the interview seriously**. If the prospective employer desires to speak to you, it means that he has interest in hiring you for the skills and abilities that you possess and have communicated through your CV. Any laxity on your part could prevent you from getting the job.
- **Have a good telephone instrument**. Whatever you hear or speak is to be communicated through the telephone instrument. Ensure that it is good, and you can hear clearly and your voice passes well.
- **Be prepared at the appointed time**. Ensure that there are no interruptions or background noises that can interfere with the interview.
- **Have the CV and documents ready**. Have your CV, the application letter and the supporting documents ready on the table before the interview. It is almost definite that the interviewer would like to check some of the facts and talk to you about them.
- **Note down special issues**. If you would like to highlight certain skills or achievements, have a list ready before the interview. You could also note down questions that you would like to be answered by the interviewer. With the paper before you, the issues could be raised at an appropriate time in the interview.
- **Speak with a smile**. Although nobody is watching you, but it is important that you are calm and have a smile on your face as you speak because that ensures a fair communication. Do not get provoked under any circumstances.

Common Interview Mistakes

Many candidates come back from an interview saying that they have had a good interview, and yet fail to get the job. There could be several reasons for this. Some pertain to the prospective employer and are beyond the understanding of a candidate. Others pertain to the candidate and must be well understood and avoided. Here are common interview mistakes people make:

- **Not arriving on time**. This is a very common reason and shows a person's disrespect for time.

- **Dressing casually**. Many candidates give an impression that they are either going on a picnic or on a party. Neither of them is right. Dress as one would when going to work.

- **Lack of knowledge**. Most candidates fail to collect information about the organisation and the job they have applied for.

- **Lack of preparation**. It may sound shocking but very few persons can introduce one's self convincingly. They lack the words and the emphasis.

- **Lack of professionalism**. Many candidates think that being informal is like being friendly: they will smoke, chew gum or tap on the file. Even during the interview, they will slouch on the chair rather than sit upright. Interviewers do not appreciate lack of professionalism.

- **Poor communication skills**. Most candidates communicate poorly. They may know what they wish to speak but fail to do so. Poor listening skills have let down millions of job aspirants. Always speak briefly and to the point.

- **Poor body language**. More than the words, all interviewers observe the body language of the candidates. Some inspire confidence others don't.

Intelligence Tests

With growing competition and the development of psychology and psychological tests to gauge individual interests, aptitudes, IQ, etc., many employers are using intelligence tests to rate prospective candidates for jobs. These tests aim at gauging an individual's mental agility, power of reasoning, comprehension, memory, etc. These tests are short, require little writing, and must be answered in a limited period. These tests are useful when the number of applicants is very high, as these help to shortlist the better ones in the lot. By no means are these tests conclusive. We cannot overlook that people who can be biased or unfair devise these tests. It is, therefore, natural that different employers attach varying degrees of importance to the results of these tests.

The IQ of a person depends upon various factors like family background, education, age, residence, personal problems, the weather, mood, and even the town from where one comes. Women have been observed to be as intelligent, but have fewer interests than men. People who spend some time on self-improvement regularly score well in these tests.

When answering these tests, it is important to avoid anxiety and tension. Before beginning the test, read the instructions carefully. Go through the test, answering the questions that you can. Do not get anxious if you cannot answer a question. Leave it, and move on to the next one. Answer all the questions that you do know and return to the difficult ones later if the time permits. If there is negative marking, avoid answering the questions you are not confident about. You will be well rewarded for tackling the test patiently.

Think it over...

Our needs are always in a hurry. They rush and hustle, no patience for anything else but fulfillment of purpose.

— *Rabindra N. Tagore*

Negotiating a Salary

Most employers specify the salary and scale of pay offered in the advertisement for the job. With greater pressures on getting the right people and the right positions, it is common to leave the matter to negotiation between the employer and the candidate. Although the employer knows what the job is worth, he may want to test the candidate's ability, and find out more about his personal aspirations and also what stage of development the candidate is passing through at that point of time.

If the candidate is already employed and just changing jobs, it should not be difficult to relate the expected salary to the one already being received. However, if this is the first job, one must make reliable inquiries and find out what the job is worth. One can find this information by studying advertisements for similar jobs or through people already working in similar positions. When asked, demand a salary accordingly. Never show a lack of decision in these matters. If the employer finds you worthy of the amount you have asked for, he will pay it. If you are capable and the difference is nominal, he will explain his stand to you.

Points to Ponder...

- The purpose of a job application is to be invited for an interview.
- One must be well prepared before going for an interview.
- The interview provides an employer the opportunity to assess the candidates' health, personality, and the skills and abilities as related to the job being offered.
- A candidate always projects a good image when he or she is aware of the essentials of an interview.
- A candidate must be well prepared to answer a variety of questions.
- To succeed, the answers to questions must always be convincing.
- When changing jobs, one must be able to explain why it is necessary.
- To judge the initiative and leadership qualities, many employers conduct group interviews.
- Outstation candidates can also be interviewed on phone before a face-to-face interview at the workplace.

- A candidate must be aware of common interview mistakes and avoid them.
- When an organisation conducts intelligence or reasoning tests before an interview, these must be answered carefully with patience.
- A prospective employee must be ready to negotiate for an appropriate salary.

Job Etiquette

It is not enough to get a job. The important thing is to make it a great success. One's livelihood, growth and self-esteem depend upon it. All appointments are initially temporary, depending upon individual performance. Only after the probation period that may range from a couple of months to a year is over that one qualifies for an appointment letter and the benefits other than the salary.

Besides the special skills and abilities that a person may have and would have been appointed to use these in one's job, everyone will need to observe what could be described as 'job etiquette'. One will need to interact with a variety of people in different positions. Besides the immediate boss, one would need to report to or work with, there will be the senior management, colleagues working at the same level and the subordinates who may be providing a variety of support services. One's success will depend upon creating good relationships at all levels at the workplace.

Besides the immediate employees of the organisation, there will be many more like the customers, the suppliers, contractual labour and others who might need one's attention and care. Positive interaction helps build good relationships. These, in turn, help provide useful experience and strengthen one's position as an employee. All this sounds easy to achieve, but it is not so. Human relationships are always very complex and building them requires a great amount of understanding, sacrifice and effort. To succeed, one will do well to understand the many factors that contribute to achieve the goals of the job in hand.

The First Job

A majority of people are at a total loss as to what to expect when they join for the first job. Anticipating the unknown, anxiety rules high. Relax. Look at it as a mutual give and take. The employer has certain needs to fulfill, and he expects to do so through the job he has given you. You need a livelihood, and you can get it by fulfilling the expectations of your employer.

To get the best from your skills and abilities, the employer will first need to acquaint you with what he expects from you. As a part of the initial orientation, he may directly introduce you to your boss who will act as your guide and mentor, and you will directly take orders and report your progress to him. As an alternative, you could be linked with a colleague who joined earlier and is doing what you will be expected to do right away or in due course of time.

No individual fits well directly into a job. Neither will you, particularly when it is your first job. Do not look at your first job as an opportunity to earn a livelihood. Instead, look at it as a place to try your skills and abilities and gain valuable experience. With all of one's knowledge, skills and abilities, one can gain experience only by doing things practically at the workplace. There is no other way to gain experience. The first thing one learns is that people do not always work the way they are taught in the classroom. There is a wide gulf between theory and practice. You will soon learn why and how.

You may be well qualified and may possess special skills, but these may not be immediately appreciated in your first job. Observe self-control. Listen to what is explained to you. This is the time when you need to use the best of your listening skills. Listen to what your employer expects of you. Pay heed to how your immediate boss expects you to do things. Do not argue. Just listen. When you work as you are told and the boss is satisfied, you could then explain how the same thing could be done better. Convince the boss later by practically doing it.

Every organisation develops its own procedures over a period. Nobody likes these to be disturbed. A certain working culture also exists in every organisation. This will need to be respected. When you join, acquaint yourself of these procedures and the culture and perform in harmony with them. As a first time employee, never challenge a procedure or the way things are done. People are reluctant to change and will accept new ideas only from those who are well established in the field, not from newcomers.

Think it over...

Man must build his culture about the complete human personality...Whatever nourishes the personality, humanizes it, refines it, deepens it, intensifies its aptitude and broadens its field of action is good; whatever sends it back to tribal patterns and limits its capacity for human co-operation and communion must be counted as bad.

— Lewis Mumford

Building Yourself

Use your first job as an opportunity to strengthen your skills and abilities by gaining insight into human behaviour at the workplace. It would be advisable to take up the first job where you can gain valuable experience even when the salary is comparatively less than your skills should attract. Experience is more important than money, and you will eventually be compensated for your efforts.

You might have earlier worked out certain career goals and also prepared a plan to achieve them. Now is the time to review the career goals. Are they realistic? Would you like to revise them? If so, in what way would you like to do it? Is the work plan you prepared practical to implement? You might want to alter it a bit to acquire newer skills or eliminate shortcomings.

Gradually build yourself through your work. Be confident. Respect your self-esteem. You must know what you stand for. You must have a set of values and beliefs. Let these be known to your family, your colleagues and others. These help strengthen one's character and turns a person into a 'brand' i.e. respected for a definite value system. Here are a few guidelines:

- Build yourself as a worthy individual with definite values and beliefs.
- Stand by your value system and commitment to work.
- Set definite goals and work towards them. Work with a definite purpose.
- Accept people as they are and not as you would want them to be. Develop lasting friendships.
- Hone your communication skills. Be a good listener. You will always be appreciated for it.

Dress Etiquette

Many people are known by the clothes they wear. Clothes tell much about a person's tastes, and his or her likes and dislikes. Clothes must be comfortable to wear, easy to care for, and elegant to look at. They must be suitable for the occasion.

At the workplace, one must wear clothes that do not distract. One must dress conservatively. Most men prefer a shirt and pant. Neckties are optional in some offices. In winters, woollen sweaters and pullovers should be sober, and not bright and gaudy. Lady employees also need to dress conservatively in office. Most prefer salwar-kamiz or sari. If used to wearing slacks, the tops must be long. Avoid low necklines or backless blouses. Jewellery should be restricted to the minimum, say, small earrings and a ring. A chain is optional. Nothing loud. Avoid heavy makeup and strong perfumes.

One must dress formally for special functions at the office. Men can wear a formal suit with necktie. Ladies can wear heavier saris or salwar-kamiz for formal wear and jewellery to match. Footwear is equally important. So are the accessories like handbags for ladies, particularly on formal occasions. Match them well.

Common Courtesies

Besides the courtesy of greeting each other every morning and evening at work, it is equally important to use the few simple words everyone learns in school. Few realise their importance. The first word is 'please'. You may be using it, but never thought how useful it is. Just add 'please' to a sentence, and observe how quickly people respond. The word adds politeness to our request. It is a symbol of goodwill.

We were also taught to say, “thank you”. However, we are shy to use these simple words in everyday life. Say “thank you” to your boss, colleagues and subordinates for whatever they do for you. They will appreciate it. “Thank you” conveys sincere gratitude. It conveys appreciation for being thoughtful. Everyone is eager to be appreciated.

Two other words that most people are hesitant to use are, “I’m sorry”. It hurts the ego every time we use them. Nobody taught us that these words could do wonders in our life. Whenever things go wrong and there is the slightest chance that it could be due to you, just say, “I’m sorry.” The problem will be sorted out. Initially, it might hurt your ego. Soon you will realise that you have gained more than what you thought you lost. To accept one’s fault is a sign of being a mature person. It is human to make mistakes. Why pretend to be God?

Two other words that can do wonders are “Excuse me”. Wherever you go, if you find that the passage to your destination is blocked, just say, “Excuse me.” The way will clear for you. To make what we say convincing, God blessed us with a smile. It costs nothing but achieves much. Say it with a smile.

Think it over...

Good manners are a part of good morals; and it is as much our duty as our interest to practise both.

— *Hunter*

Office Etiquette

Every business or organization operates from an office, which needs to fulfill a definite purpose. This is not possible without discipline. Some rules are written. Many are not. Those which are not written come within working style or customs adopted by the organization. These become a part of office etiquette.

Good etiquette and manners contribute to make an office a congenial place to work. Here are a few simple guidelines:

- The employer is paying you for the time you spend at the office. Respect time – your own and that of others. When you use time for any other purpose than office work, you are stealing time. If you have urgent work, there are provisions for leave.

- Every office has a working culture pertaining to handling of documents, files, office equipment and stationery. It is necessary that every evening the table is clear, the documents have been filed and files have been placed in the cabinets. The stationery must be back in the table drawer.

- Midday tea or coffee is served in some offices. Remember that this should not be an occasion for a friendly chat.

- Toilets are provided in offices as a convenience. Leave the toilet in a condition that you would like to find it when you want to use it.

- Every job requires dealing with people having different temperaments. Observe self-restraint and patience in dealing with them. Tact and patience can be useful tools.

- The telephone in an office is likely to be misused. The management never likes the office telephones to be used for personal use. It is good etiquette not to use the phone for outgoing calls without permission. Incoming calls should be received for an urgent message and not on routine basis.

- There is break down of discipline when employees misuse office equipment like calculators, typewriters, fax machines, computers, printers and Photostat machines. Office furniture is another item of abuse. Avoid this misuse.

- Office vehicles are for limited use only. Do not misuse your privileges. Similarly, entertainment allowances are strictly for professional use.

- When men and women work in the same office, there must be courtesy and decency. Everyone has a responsibility to fulfill. Personal and professional activities must not be mixed. Treat each other as a member of a team.

- Every office has a definite policy regarding working additional time. If lady employees need to stay late, they must be provided transport to return to their homes.

Telephone Etiquette

Perhaps nothing has connected as many people together as the telephone. Business houses have a telephone on every desk. Documents are transmitted through fax machines connected to the telephone line. The Internet connected through the telephone has brought the world to every home and office. It has become possible to send messages and pictures, and even chat with people around the world. A vast storehouse of knowledge is now available through the Internet.

These developments have made it necessary to maintain etiquette and good manners on the telephone. Here are a few guidelines that can be useful:

- A telephone is a device. Understand how it works. Learn how to use keys like mute, pause, flash and redial. Read the telephone booklet. Use the facility to store telephone numbers.
- Understand how a telephone is given a number. For example, if your number is 271 1234, the exchange number is 271, and your number is 1234.
- Every city too has a number. For example, Delhi's code is 011, Mumbai's code is 022, Kolkata's code is 033 and Chennai's code is 044. This way, every city has its own code.
- A number also identifies every country. The number 91 identifies India.
- One must maintain a personal telephone directory to record the names and telephone numbers of the persons one usually needs to speak to.
- For emergency use, the numbers of the hospital, fire brigade, railway station, bus terminal, police station and your doctor must be on record.
- Use the telephone only when you need to. You must know whom you want to talk to and what you want to convey.

- When you get the dialed number, immediately disclose your identity by saying, "I am Sam. Could I please speak to...?" This way you have immediately conveyed who you are and whom you would like to speak to. If the person is available, he or she will come on line.
- When you dial a business number, the receptionist will greet you saying, "Good morning. This is ABC Ltd. Can I help you?" You could then disclose your identity and the person you would like to speak to. If you desire some information, the receptionist would connect you with the appropriate person. If the person is not available, the receptionist will request you to call later or leave your number.
- When an answering machine is connected to the telephone, you may hear a voice saying, "This is Jones' residence. We are not at home. Could you please leave your message?" At this point you could just say, "I am Joan calling. Could you please ring me at 323 1234? Thank you."
- When you dial a number from a place where a private exchange is installed, as in some homes, in offices and hotels, you will first need to dial a number like '0' or '9', or even some other number before you hear the dial tone. Inquire the number from the owner of the phone. In hotels, it is noted in the directory of services provided in every room.
- Telephones at railway stations and airports may be connected to a computer. Follow instructions to obtain the desired information.

- When you order supplies on the telephone, identify yourself, the address and the telephone number you are speaking from. To ensure that it is not a bogus call by a prankster, the service provider rings back immediately to confirm the name of the caller and the order.

- When dialing international numbers, it is good manners to check the time of the country where you wish to connect the call. It may be daytime here, but could be the middle of the night in the country you call. You could disturb the person at an odd hour.

- When a fax number does not respond, dial the number and request that the fax machine may be switched on.

- When speaking on the phone, it is your voice that creates an impression at the other end. Speak courteously. Be polite. Answer the call gently. Never use harsh language. While speaking on the phone, never converse with others simultaneously. Modern telephone instruments are sensitive. They pick up voices from a distance. Sometimes it can create misunderstandings.

- Sometimes you may get a wrong number. Say "sorry" and close the call.

Think it over...

In conversation use some, but not too much ceremony; it teaches others to be courteous, too. Demeanors are commonly paid back in their own coin.

— *Fuller*

Mobile Phone Etiquette

Mobile phones have changed the way people think and work. These have connected people in the remotest areas almost around the clock. It is necessary that people must observe good manners and etiquette when using mobile phones. Here are a few guidelines about using mobile phones:

- People subscribe to mobile phone service for personal convenience. You have no right to impose upon it. When you want to speak to a person, first try the landline number. Dial the mobile phone number only in an emergency.

- Keep the conversation short and to the point. If the message is short, use SMS (short message service).

- Avoid disturbing people in restaurants, cinema halls, and public meetings.

- Mobile phones keep ringing at the wrong places. It is good manners to keep the ringer off when you are in a public place.

- When you respond to a call in a public place, remember that speaking even in hushed tones can be disturbing to others. Excuse yourself; move to a place where you can speak without disturbing others.

Carrying a mobile phone is useful when you are away from home. You can be traced in case of an emergency. You can call in case of need. However, it is dangerous to speak on a phone and drive at the same time. If it is urgent and you need to speak, stop the vehicle and speak.

Email Etiquette

With computers in every home and office, people now communicate through emails. Even within offices, inter-office communications are through emails. This has cut down upon writing conventional memos and letters. However, there is now the need to observe email etiquette. It would be useful to follow these courtesies:

- Unless you check your mailbox every day, do not give your email address to everyone. It makes no sense if mail is not responded to.
- When writing emails, most people do away with conventional practices like using capital letters, ensuring grammatical correctness, using proper punctuation and similar usage. They use abbreviations to write messages quickly.
- Write short messages in small case. Using 'all capitals' in the message is like shouting. Use this only when you need to shout at the recipient.
- When sending attachments, ensure that they are not large. They can choke the recipient's mailbox.
- Do not send any unsolicited mail. The recipient will not appreciate it.
- Do not pass email addresses of your friends and acquaintances to others without their permission.
- Send mail only to concerned persons. Do not send copies to everyone you *think* would find the mail interesting.

- Do not indulge in creating chains, or forwarding chain mail. No one has ever been blessed by luck or received money by sending mail. Additional mail increases the Internet traffic, slows down the services and irritates the recipients.

- Do not open attached mail received from persons you do not know. Many attachments are known to carry virus that can cause loss of valuable data.

Office Gossip

It is natural for office colleagues to get together and converse with each other. All conversations do not pertain to work only. Generally, conversations tend to drift and become personal. One gets down to talking about one's families, hopes and aspirations. Slowly it can lead to familiarity, and one gets down to talking about one's colleagues. Everything said or heard may not be sensible. It may arise from small incidents that may be misinterpreted and blown out of proportion, making it cheap gossip. This can be dangerous for the individuals and the office in general because it can lead to misunderstandings and personal ill will. One should not mix office work and gossip. It is best to keep office relationships formal and avoid conversations that can lead to unnecessary personal remarks or aspersions. A new entrant into an organisation should strive to maintain professional relationships and not make them personal.

Cultural Differences

India is a vast country with diverse cultures, customs and outlook. This is clearly visible in all organisations where workers come from all regions, speaking a variety of languages and practicing different religions and beliefs. With rapid development and job opportunities, workers are moving in from other countries also. This has made the workplace a meeting ground of all cultures. Except for common working goals, one is bound to come across great variations in language, habits, food and perception. This can sometimes make things difficult, but at the same time, it provides opportunities to learn from each other. When working in such circumstances, one needs to learn to accept people as they are. Comparisons can be odious, and criticism can be harmful. One must respect each other's way of life. One must be professional in dealing with others at the workplace.

Think it over...

Dignity consists not in possessing honours, but in the consciousness that we deserve them.

— *Aristotle*

Dignity of Labour

It is surprising how individuals look at different kinds of work. Even within the office some employees consider responsibilities that involve some physical work as menial and avoid it. This is more so in developing countries within some cultures than in the developed nations where everyone is willing to pitch in. This attitude has given rise to terms like blue-collar or white-collar jobs. Some people hesitate even to offer a glass of water or a cup of tea to a visitor, considering it a menial responsibility. Others feel shy to wipe the top of their working table or to empty the dustbin lying under the table. In India, we could say that we have carried this attitude from the time the British ruled the country.

Everyone who has such an attitude needs to be reminded that it is wrong. All kinds of work are honourable and good. We must honour the dignity of labour. In any workplace, everyone must be willing to do all kinds of work connected with the particular field of activity. A self-employed storeowner who has ten persons to help him does not hesitate to pack goods for a customer. Why should an office employee feel shy to wipe one's own table in the office? Why should one hesitate to offer a glass of water to a visitor? How people look at different kinds of work is a matter of attitude. Everyone serving an organisation needs to guard against it.

Office Meetings

All kinds of meetings are held in offices every day. In terms of manpower, these meetings cost large sums of money. Some of these meetings are useful. Others may achieve nothing for several reasons. When organizing or attending meetings, you will do well to remember the following:

- Is the meeting necessary? A meeting must have a definite purpose to achieve.

- Has the meeting been appropriately announced? Have all the participants been invited? Has the agenda been circulated? Have physical arrangements been made for the meeting? All these are important considerations.

- Meetings must start and end on time. Lack of punctuality exemplifies disrespect for other people's time. Discuss the agenda item-wise. All relevant material pertaining to the points of discussion must be made available.

- If there is a telephone in the room, disconnect it during the meeting. Request the participants to have their cell phones switched off.

- If refreshments are to be served, they must be served either before the meeting or after it. There should be no interruptions during the meeting.

- The minutes of the meeting must be recorded. They can be circulated later as a follow-up.

Smoking on the Job

Smoking is prohibited in public places like airports and railway stations, cinema halls and theatres, hospitals, libraries and several other places. It is also prohibited in public conveyances like trains and buses. Many business houses also prohibit smoking in their premises. There are specific reasons for these restrictions. All smokers must observe them.

It is best to avoid smoking on the job. Even if smoking is permitted in your office, seek the permission of the persons in the vicinity. Without your being aware of it, a person could be allergic to smoke. Elderly people are especially sensitive to this problem. Use an ashtray when you smoke. Put off the stub when you stop smoking. Do not leave it lit.

Drinking at Work

Social drinking is on the increase amongst men and women. Some drink moderately and stay within limits. A few who drink indiscriminately end up creating a nuisance for themselves and others. Drinking is totally prohibited in workplaces even after office hours. It is equally important that one should not drink heavily at home and come the next morning to office with a hangover. One must appreciate that alcohol is a drug. Like other drugs, the sensitivity to alcohol varies from one person to another. Drinking is best avoided. If drinks are served at an office party, one should drink moderately. Do not mix drinks. Sometimes they can have a bad effect. Do not let anybody force you to a drink. "One for the road" is a folly. People drink for pleasure. Do not let it become displeasure–for you and others!

Think it over...

It is a common law of nature, which no time will ever change, that superiors shall rule their inferiors.

— *Dyonysius*

Keeping the Boss Happy

The immediate concern of every employee is to keep the boss happy. There are innumerable stories about what people do to keep the boss happy but many of them are in lighter vein. Every boss has certain amount of work to be done, and nothing pleases one more than to see it completed. Even the boss needs to grow at work, and this is possible only when he can prove himself efficient to complete his work and be prepared for more responsibility.

You can make it happen through the work assigned to you. A boss is a human and so are you. To give your work a personal touch here are a few guidelines:

- Indulge in sensible conversation. Talk only as much as is necessary. Talking too much tends to make one lean towards familiarity, which may not be the right thing.

- Be a part of the solution and not the problem. Everyone has problems and one is bound to refer them to the boss. When you take a problem to him, also take some possible solutions which will lighten his burden.

- Say "No" to the impossible. An efficient employee is always burdened with more work than others. Sometimes it becomes impossible to handle it all. Do not hesitate to tell him so. He will understand it.

- Go all the way. Nothing pleases a boss more than a person, who meets the deadlines, completes the work, speaks up to give suggestions, and is forever ready to share a helping hand or a moment of fun with others.

- Be a willing learner. Everyone makes mistakes and so will you. Don't pass the buck. Accept your fault and say, "Sorry". It is foolish to make the same mistake twice. It is wisdom to learn from one's mistakes.

Team Spirit

Everyone is an individual in his or her own right and joins an organisation as such. Work is also allocated to everyone on an individual basis, and it is assessed that way also. However, it is necessary that when one joins an organisation, one becomes a part of the team that consists of all the workers. One does not need to be invited to the team. Everyone should look at it that way. Experience has shown that this team spirit improves the productivity of the organisation and also of each individual worker. All that needs to be done is to be concerned about each other and the contribution one makes through work to make the organisation great. If a person is over-worked perhaps others could share the burden. In the same way, if a person is on leave, the work should not be allowed to suffer. Others should volunteer to keep the organisation in good shape. The team spirit encourages everyone to grow at the workplace.

Managing Stress

No job is free of stress. One realizes this only when one gets into a particular situation. In a job, one needs to commute, work for a set number of hours, abide by the discipline of the organisation and at the end of the day have something to show as attained. When one goes through this routine day after day, a certain amount of stress builds up. One copes with physical stress through rest. However, the emotional stress that builds up gradually needs to be handled with greater care. Most organisations are becoming aware of this problem and are suggesting yoga, meditation, exercise and other ways to cope with it. The new aspirants need to be as cautious about this problem as their senior colleagues. Work stress is a major problem being faced by the modern society and needs to be addressed in harmony with individual personalities. Don't ignore it.

Points to Ponder...

- It is necessary for every employee to maintain job etiquette at the workplace.
- Every newcomer in an organisation needs to learn the culture developed at the workplace over a period.
- In a job one gets a new insight into human behaviour at the workplace. This helps one gain valuable experience.
- One must dress appropriately at the workplace.
- Common courtesies of everyday life help remove small irritations from human relationships at the workplace.
- Many unwritten rules form a part of office etiquette and culture.
- The office telephone connects people quickly but is often misused by the employees.
- Your mobile phone should not be a nuisance for others.
- Email etiquette makes communication smoother and swifter.
- Office gossip can lead to serious consequences.
- One should not overlook cultural differences at the workplace.

- Accept responsibilities at the workplace with dignity and respect.
- Unless well organised and managed, office meetings could be a waste of time and effort.
- Smoking and drinking at the workplace are best avoided.
- Act responsible to keep the boss happy.
- Be a part of the larger team to succeed at the workplace.
- Manage workplace stress through positive relaxation activities.

Giving Your Best Performance

Finding a good job is important. Knowing how to fulfill the responsibilities of the job is equally necessary. The ultimate aim should be to give one's best performance. The majority argue, why would one not do so? Why would one not perform well? The simple answer to this question is that people who do jobs are not machines. Only machines can be expected to perform to a particular capacity. When a machine goes wrong and the productivity suffers, the worn out parts can be replaced and the optimum performance attained. Those who do jobs are human beings. Like all others they have their frailties and, therefore, performance varies from one person to another, depending upon a variety of factors.

One must appreciate that every job carries with it a definite responsibility, which must be fulfilled. While on one hand, there is the employer who is eager to have the responsibilities fulfilled, on the other hand there is the employee who is there to fulfill this responsibility for remuneration, which is the source of his or her livelihood. Both the employer and the employee have needs, which apparently are easy to fulfill. However, the employer-employee relationship depends upon human frailties. This, in turn, influences employee performance.

Unfortunately, two out of every five persons are doing the wrong kind of work. We cannot expect them to put in their best performance. Caught in a vicious circle, people find it difficult to change course. As a result, we see too much mediocrity in every field. People are just working from 8.00 a.m. to 5.00 p.m. out of compulsion and the performance suffers, affecting the interests of the employer and the employee. To succeed, performing to one's best ability is very important. One must understand how this can be achieved.

Leave the Past Behind

Too many people live in the past. They find it difficult to forget past incidents, shortcomings and failures. They take up a new job, move into new environment and have a whole life to live ahead of them, but like little children, they keep looking behind at their past faults. They refuse to grow up and move on. Can they perform under such circumstances? Setbacks in life should be used as opportunities to gain experience and learn new things in life. They are really stepping stones to success, and not obstacles. The difference lies in the way one looks at the situation. If some things are still holding you back, now is the time to change the way you look at them. It is all in the mind. Change the way you think, and you will be ready to move ahead.

If you want to get ahead in your job and life, you need to leave your past behind. If you find that difficult, it is time to evaluate the situation and find ways to get over what has gone by. Ask yourself some simple questions. What is it that I am unhappy about? Is it my personality, my education or my family circumstances? Are some of my past failures still haunting me? Do I fear something I am not sure about? Can I define these fears in exact terms? Note down these questions on paper and answer them. Take your own time in writing the answers, but do it honestly. These answers will help you assess how serious a problem is.

In a majority of cases, one imagines a problem to be far more serious than it really is. Only when you write the damages that can accrue that they begin to lose their sting and the reality emerges. The damages may finally appear small and insignificant, but while you are at the exercise do not ignore them. Against each problem write down what is the worst that could happen. Now ask yourself if you could prevent some of the damage. List ways to do so. Prepare a plan to execute the likely solutions that you have worked out. Soon you will emerge the victor. The problems of the past will be behind you. Always remind yourself that there is no problem that does not have a solution. Choose to be a part of the solution, and not that of the problem.

Your Personality

Take a new look at your personality. You assessed your strengths and weaknesses earlier. However, when you get a job, reassess yourself once again. It is popular for people to carry out a SWOT analysis where each of the four letters S, W, O and T represent the words strengths, weaknesses, opportunities and threats. You will do well to consider each of them in relation to the job you have taken up:

- **Strengths.** Do your skills and abilities match those that are required to perform the responsibilities of the job? Can you put your skills and abilities to the best use in the present job, or are you using them partially only? The answers can help you assess the correct utilization of your strengths.

- **Weaknesses**. Do you feel that you lack some skills or are unable to cope with the responsibilities of the job? The lack of these skills could make you feel inadequate to cope with the situation. Can you make up for these weaknesses by acquiring the necessary skills in due time? If so, by when? These could improve your performance significantly.

- **Opportunities**. What new opportunities are coming your way through the job? You could be gaining experience, improving your communication skills or finding it easy to network with a variety of people at the workplace. Every job provides opportunities, and these could be useful for your future growth. How can you use these opportunities to your advantage?

- **Threats**. What new threats have emerged from your having accepted the job? Every new situation involves change, which can be threatening because of the unknown elements. The job could require one to travel excessively, to keep away from the family or go to places where common living comforts are not available. The job could also offer competition from new people.

With an analysis of one's feelings on the lines suggested above, it is possible to look at the job from a realistic perspective so that one gains from the experience and uses it to move up the ladder of success. Periodic personal assessment in one's job helps a person to keep on track. It is a necessary tool to move towards long-term goals.

Think it over...

I never did anything worth doing by accident, nor did any of my inventions come by accident.

— Thomas A. Edison

Career Goals

Would you sit in a boat and let it take you wherever the current takes it, or would you like to steer and direct it to your destination? Taking up a job is very much like getting on to a boat. Once you know that you have got on to the right boat, it is time to direct it carefully. You need to know where you are going and why. To make this possible, you will need to understand the basics of goal setting and also why it is necessary to set short-term and long-term goals.

To be effective, a goal must be:

- **Measurable**. A goal must be tangible and visible to be accepted as an achievement. If it cannot be measured, it cannot be a goal. When setting a goal, one must be clear as to what one desires to attain.

- **Challenging**. A goal can be challenging only when one decides to achieve more than what one is doing presently. It is not enough to set a goal that simply aims at good performance in your present position. That is not challenging enough to take you ahead. It must aim at higher positions.

- **Achievable**. A goal must be achievable. It is good to aim high. However, if the targets are beyond your current circumstances, you cannot achieve them. This discourages a person, and one withdraws the efforts to return to the comfort zone. Progress halts thereafter.

❖ **Time-bound**. If a goal is not time-bound, it cannot be an effective goal. Can you play a game of football without any time limit? How do you decide who wins? When a goal is time-bound, one works harder to achieve it. In school we learn the value of time. We must qualify in each class in a year otherwise we fail. We need to remember that at the workplace also.

❖ **Shared**. A goal must be shared so that it becomes a group responsibility. Irrespective whether a goal is set at home or the workplace, if it involves other people, it must be shared with them. This way you will not be let down. There will be many goals at the workplace that involve several people. They must be involved when the goal is agreed upon, a plan to achieve it is prepared and is finally executed.

Write the Goals

To have effective goals, they must be written on paper. If more than one person is involved with a particular goal, each partner must have it written on paper. You must write what you desire to achieve and how it is to be done. You must also write the timeframe as to what is to be achieved when. When a goal is adopted only in the memory, it is soon forgotten when newer thoughts fill the mind. Life is multifaceted. There will be several goals and sub-goals to remember. There will also be many goals pertaining to other aspects of life. The only way to ensure success is to have every goal written down. You could have a small notebook to record the goals that you set for yourself and call it, "My Path to Success".

Goals and Flexibility

A goal cannot be flexible. If it is flexible, it cannot be a goal. For example, in most examinations marks are scored on the basis of a perfect score of 100. This means that for every student, the goal is to score 100 marks. If a majority score between 50 and 60, would it be fair to scale down the perfect score from 100 to 80 to help the students to attain a higher percentage? Goals should not be tampered with. It may not be possible to attain it at the first try. However, one must keep trying. With practice, one performs better. To attain one's goals, one must improve skills and abilities, and not make goals flexible. The only area where one could employ flexibility is in the methods used to attain a goal. If one method does not work, another one could be used to achieve a particular goal.

Long-term and Short-term Goals

A goal needs to be time bound. However, this does not mean that all goals must be completed in the same amount of time. Some goals can be attained at one sitting, some in a day, a week, a month, or even in a year. Others may take much longer. In setting goals, one needs to set both long-term and short-term goals. They must be set according to need.

For example, Eric Samuel always desired to be the head of a marketing department of a company. He cannot attain that position soon after qualifying from a management school. This would, therefore, be his long-term goal. To reach that position, he would have to rise step by step from lower positions like sales supervisor to area sales manager, regional sales manager and sales manager. Each position requires a certain level of knowledge, experience, integrity and dedication. It becomes necessary to set goals to gain the skills and abilities for the position through personal discipline, study and hard work. It will be equally important to set goals to give the best performance. This would be possible through short-term goals. One can work through short-term goals to attain the long-term goals. All successful people have done it that way.

Review the Career Plan

Whether a person is self-employed or doing a job, one needs to plan to succeed. Without planning, one could be left behind. Earlier, we discussed how to plan a career so that one knows which way to go. With a job in hand and a feel of what it takes to succeed, it is necessary that one must review the plan periodically to ensure that one is on the right track. With a timeframe to follow, one can review the progress that is being made. If there are any problems, one can change course by adopting new methods to attain the goals. With a SWOT analysis carried out, it becomes easier to perform better and move ahead.

Think it over...

Planning, as the pursuit of a conscious aim, is exclusively a human trait and it develops fully with the progress of civilization.

— *Abraham Lincoln*

Job Expectations and Fulfillment

One needs to take up a job because the remuneration is a source of livelihood. However, one does not work for money alone; there are other needs that must also be fulfilled to provide true job satisfaction and motivation to perform well. To move ahead, one needs to evaluate the situation periodically. Here are a few questions and guidelines that can help you understand the situation:

- Do I find the job interesting? You will find it as interesting as the interest you take in the activities involved.

- Is it an experience in learning? The first job should be an experience in learning. One learns how organisations operate, how people respond to everyday activities and how one can get ahead in life.

- Is the job challenging? If you find it challenging, it means that you are learning at the workplace. Challenges prepare one for greater things in life.

- Is your job offering you opportunities to network with new people? When you meet new people, more opportunities open up. You begin to see new areas of growth and progress.

- Are you using your skills at work? When you use your skills and abilities, they become better and the performance improves with them.

- Do you feel stressed at the end of the day? A certain amount of physical stress is normal at the end of the day, but this is soon released through rest. If your work leaves you tense, you need to make further adjustments to accept the situation.

Learning on the Job

There is no end to learning at the workplace. Earlier, one learnt only through experience. Presently, many organisations are maintaining facilities to regularly upgrade the skills of the employees. Those who do not have in-house training facilities hire firms who specialise in training activities. One must take full advantage of these facilities to get ahead at the workplace. One quality that all employers like in their employees is their desire to learn new skills and hone the existing ones through upgrading of knowledge.

Communication Skills

In any job, good communication skills are an asset. To succeed, one must be able to communicate well. One may be knowledgeable, experienced and wise, but unless one is able to communicate effectively with others, nothing worthwhile can be attained. Both spoken and written communications are important. One can communicate feelings and emotions in other ways also. One's presence on a particular occasion communicates a message. One also communicates through silence. It is a tool to introspect or talk to one's self. Silence is also used to punish another person by not talking to him or her.

People also communicate through gestures, clothes and even makeup. Women spend much time in dressing and makeup to communicate that they are pretty. Fragrances also convey a message. Body gestures convey more than words. People speak with their eyes. Some convey a message through silence and a smile. Others convey disapproval without speaking a word. One can see when people are happy, sad, angry, disheartened, disapproving, or whatever. Facial expressions and the body language tell much. One must communicate positive body language. Through it one is able to communicate the level of confidence. When negotiating, people gain advantage over others through their ability to interpret body language.

In the modern context, good speaking skills are an asset. They add to one's effectiveness and help promote leadership qualities to come forth. Equally important is the ability to listen attentively. Generally, people speak more than they listen. One cannot be persuasive in such circumstances. No one likes to be ignored. The moment one realizes that the other person is not listening one gets switched off. Listening skills are like other skills, and one must learn them as a part of career growth. Good listening skills are as important as speaking persuasively or writing effectively.

Think it over...

The more a person is able to direct his life consciously, the more he can use time for constructive benefits.

— *Rollo May*

Managing Time

Time is God's gift to everyone–the rich and the poor, the educated and the illiterate. God gives time without distinction between individuals, their caste, colour or creed. It does not matter where one lives, or what religion or faith one follows. God gives time equally to everyone.

Time flows at a steady speed, neither too fast nor too slow. It flows from the future and recedes to the past, moving to eternity without a break. How well a person uses time is a personal matter. While many learn to utilise it to their complete satisfaction, others just let it fritter away, leaving them frustrated. People don't need to work harder. They need to work smarter. A capable person has time for everything – for the family, his vocation, the society and for himself! It is all a matter of how a person uses one's time.

Good time management is no mystery. One can learn it like any other management skill. A person who desires to achieve much in a short period needs to make effective time management a part of his or her vocational activity.

Good Relationships

The ability to get along well with people can help a person to rise to great heights of success. People who enjoy top positions in organisations are not there only because of their business or professional skills, but because of their ability to understand and get along well with people.

Every job involves dealing with people. The most important person one needs to satisfy and keep happy is the employer. There will also be other senior members of the staff, colleagues and subordinates. Besides these there will be customers, clients and suppliers who visit the organisation regularly. Each will require different kind of handling. Dealing with people appears to be very easy, but it is not so. It is one of the most complex activities at the workplace. While it offers a lot of opportunities to network with people and get ahead in life, dealing with people offers the greatest of all challenges. To succeed, one must acquire skills. This requires a lifetime of learning. The sooner one begins, the better it is.

A very important aspect that needs to be understood is that today both men and women work together on equal terms. While in some cultures men continue to dominate the scene, but almost in every field we have women who are equally qualified as men to lead the organisations. Lady presidents are at the helm of affairs in many organisations. When men and women work together, it is necessary that office etiquette must be at its best. The relationships must be professional with due respect given to all concerned. At the workplace, both men and women are prone to develop relationships, which may be looked down upon by the management and also the colleagues. Many organisations have definite written rules about such matters and one must abide by them. Some organisations do not employ couples. They prefer to have only the husband or the wife working for the organisation.

Working as a Team

Organisations are getting bigger and more competitive. Although individual responsibility continues to be important in every job, people work in groups or teams, each team being responsible for a particular activity. We cannot overlook that the work contributed by every individual makes a team respond like a chain. It is as strong as its weakest link. In times of stress, the link breaks giving rise to confusion and failure. Therefore, as a team member it is important that everyone must fulfill one's share of responsibility in attaining the goal before the team. To succeed, one must be clear about the goal to be attained, the deadlines and the responsibilities assigned to each team member. In a team, when a member is unable to fulfill his or her responsibility, other members of the team carry the workload through without a word of complaint.

Working as a team empowers individuals to perform much better than what can be expected of them when working alone. Teamwork does not require that the members of a team must give up their individuality or live a common lifestyle; it rather depends upon every team member to contribute one's best in attaining a mutually agreed upon goal. While everyone lives their own life, the common goal ties them together, enabling everyone to perform better. Successful teamwork encourages individuals to be more responsible, develop a vision towards a better tomorrow and gives every team member a feeling of group ownership that promotes productivity. Being a good team member is the first step to growing in a job in any organisation.

Office Politics

Relationships are always complex. With many men and women working together and each person looking at things from his or her perspective, there are bound to be different ways of looking at things. People cannot resist giving opinions, and we have gossip doing rounds in every office. We discussed it earlier. With marked differences of opinions amongst workers at different levels of work, the gossip takes the shape of office politics. Some people are manipulative, while others are not. When things go wrong, it is the simple-hearted innocent people who get into trouble. All office workers need to steer clear from office politics because they do nobody any good. Newcomers especially need to be careful. They can get into trouble for no fault. Always remember that you are at the workplace to do a job. Keep your mind focused on how you can best fulfill your responsibilities. Avoid getting involved in any kind of office politics through stray remarks or opinions.

Think it over...

We have too many people who live without working, and we have altogether too many who work without living.

— Charles R. Brown

Workplace and the Home

With a fulltime job to attend to the whole day, with additional time spent on commuting between the home and office, it is natural for a person to spend lesser time at home. This can greatly influence relationships within the home and a person may experience a new kind of pressure on this account. With a job to do and fulfill the responsibilities involved, it would be necessary to create a balance between the home and the office. This is particularly so with women workers who may be trying to do a job and bring up small children simultaneously. Some employers are considerate. With use of computers and the Internet, rather than let go a talented young person, many employers are now willing to let some of them work from their homes, visiting the office occasionally. Many employers are also willing to consider flexible working hours where the salary is linked to the amount of work done, partially at home and the rest at the workplace. Both men and women may have different kinds of problems pertaining to the home and the workplace, but what is necessary is that there must be a reasonable balance between the two for a person to be able to put in the best performance and succeed.

Remaining Focused

To succeed in a job, it is necessary to remain focused on the responsibilities of the job. The moment a person's attention is diverted to other activities at the workplace or outside, one begins to slip much to the annoyance of the employer. People often argue why a person would shift his or her attention to other activities other than those of the job, but it happens. Every organisation has workers who are not focused on their responsibilities. This is a matter of great concern to every employer. When the problem is on a larger scale, organisations begin to slip and the employers are compelled to resort to retrenchment. Those who are the least focused and not contributing sufficiently by way of fulfilling their responsibilities are always the first to go. In the developed countries where salaries are high, workers live under the constant threat of being relieved because of lack of efficiency and focus on what needs to be done. The highly competitive environment is forcing all employers to adopt the policy of retaining only the focused workers.

Absenteeism

Employers pay the workers for doing work and not for sitting at home. It is admitted that everyone needs to live and also relax to contribute the best of one's skills and abilities. A weekly holiday is provided to all the workers almost everywhere around the world. In many organisations and countries, people work to a five-day week allowing them two complete days to de-stress, spend time with their family and complete their household work. It annoys the employers when workers are absent from work. The members of the team are burdened with additional responsibility and the productivity in general suffers. Employers look down upon workers who are prone to absenteeism even when he or she is not paid for the days they do not work. In most organisations, there are definite rules for casual and sick leave. Some organisations encourage their workers by paying additional salary to those who do not avail of these privileges.

Promotions

In many government jobs, in the defense services and the police promotions are often linked with time spent in that particular field. One gets promoted to the next level on completing a particular period of service. Increments in salary are also calculated on an annual basis until one reaches the top scale. Further growth depends upon rising to the next higher level. Special promotions depend upon outstanding work done beyond the normal routine.

In private organisations, promotions depend upon the level of responsibility a person can handle. Beginning at the lowest level, one is promoted on the basis of experience gained and new skills learnt. Salary increments are given on an annual basis. Commercial organisations are very conscious of productivity and profitability. Promotions depend upon individual skills and abilities. People also seek promotions through job changing, moving from one position in an organisation to the next higher position in another organisation. Some persons are fortunate to leapfrog to much higher positions through their ability to handle greater responsibilities than others.

Changing Jobs

Young people are impatient to grow at work. It is not long before they begin to get restive to look for better opportunities elsewhere. The remuneration from the first job may not be what one would consider oneself worthy of, but the purpose is not only to be compensated for the hard work one may put in, but also to gain valuable experience on the job. This is not available in colleges and universities where one is taught the basics and one learns the rest at the workplace. The first job may not provide an outlet for all of one's skills and abilities. It should, however, offer opportunities for honing these skills and be a stepping stone for future growth and progress.

One should not change a job just for the sake of it. Employers are never happy about those who change jobs. When this is done too often, employers consider the person unstable and avoid him or her. When there is a better opening, one must consider it carefully. Consider the advantages and disadvantages of changing the job. Many times the increase in fringe benefits may only be illusory. To justify a change of jobs, there should be an increased salary, more responsibility, better chances of promotion, and lots of job satisfaction. If you can get these in another job, only then would it be worthwhile to change your present job.

Think it over...

Happily, our self-image can be changed at any point in our lives.

— *Richard Robertiello*

Building a Positive Image

The modern trend is not to have products that are known by the corporate name, but to develop a "brand" name for each product over a period. Each brand offers a specialty. In times of need, companies do not sell their manufacturing facilities but sell a "brand" name and all that goes with it.

In the same way, when people join work, particularly specialized work, they begin to build an image by which they are known in their field. To understand it better, look at the images politicians create. In the same way, it is for all public to observe the images created by sportsmen and those in the entertainment industry. People get to be known both for their strengths and weaknesses.

These examples have been cited because they are easy to observe and understand. Work in other fields is not open to public view, but the principles work in the same way. In every workplace, there are key people one can depend upon for service. It is because of the positive image that they have created over a period through good work practices. It is immaterial how important a responsibility may or may not be, but one does create an image at the workplace. Even in a retail store, one seeks the attention of a particular salesperson because he or she has an image for providing better service.

In the same way, as one works at a job, one develops an image that sends out both positive and negative vibrations. One must make an effort to ensure that the positive vibrations dominate and create a positive image of one's skills and abilities and the way one handles responsibility. It is the first step towards growing in one's career. With time, as one gains experience and additional skills, one is well set for a purposeful life.

Points to Ponder...

- The ultimate aim at the workplace should be to give off one's best performance.
- Past setbacks and failures should not hold a person from providing the best service.
- To perform well, one must review and assess personal growth at the workplace.
- Setting career goals helps promote efficiency and achievement.
- Both long-term and short-term goals must be written down.

- Using career goals as the foundation, one must review the career plan.
- Besides financial benefits, one must assess job satisfaction and personal motivation levels.
- Learning at the workplace should be a continuous process.
- Optimum performance depends greatly upon effective communication, time management and human relations at the workplace.
- Working as a team helps produce more than one can achieve individually.
- Always keep away from office gossip and politics.
- There must be a fair balance between the home and the workplace.
- Remaining focused on one's responsibilities promotes growth.
- Absenteeism and promotions do not go together.
- Changing jobs must be considered in great depth.
- To grow at the workplace build a positive "brand" image.

A Super Job

Everyone desires to have a super job – a job where one's skills and abilities match the responsibilities that need to be fulfilled, the employer is congenial and considerate, the working environment is friendly, and one is able to live a balanced life where there is time for everything. You could also call it a dream job. However, the important question is: How many succeed in getting a super job?

In our journey in search for a super job, we have observed that before one can desire for anything one must prepare oneself through discipline and education to acquire the necessary skills, understand the employment situation as related to one's needs, communicate effectively and convince the prospective employer and finally give off one's best performance. We have also observed that a super job depends upon two people – the employer who has a need to get something done, and the employee who has the necessary skills to fulfill the needs of the employer. The remuneration for the work depends upon supply and demand in a particular setup and locality.

A good employer understands his own needs and those of his employees. He wants to be fair and kind, but his feelings are related to how well his needs are being fulfilled by the employee. This is totally within the control of the employee and not that of the employer. Just as one started the journey in search of a super job, one will need to continue to strive to find out the best ways to keep the employer satisfied. Situations at the workplace continue to change because life is dynamic. What is relevant today may not be so tomorrow. Therefore, a capable employee is forever on the lookout to acquire the necessary skills to cope with the change and continue one's journey towards success.

The Ideal Job

An ideal job is not where one needs to work the least and get the best remuneration. No reasonable father would offer such a job even to his own son. If one does that, it would not be offering a job but a gift to the son. The remuneration is always linked with the skills of an employee and the responsibilities that need to be fulfilled.

Another important aspect is that what may be an ideal job to one person may not be so to another. Every individual gauges situations consistent with one's perception of a situation. The perception depends upon a person's background, education and experience. Therefore, the individual's perception is bound to change with growing knowledge and experience. Yet everyone wants to know what makes a job ideal. What are the criteria one should use to evaluate the job? Here are a few guidelines to help you appreciate what an ideal job would mean to most people. A job must meet the following needs:

- **Job satisfaction**. One must derive personal satisfaction in doing a job. Two out of every five persons do not derive satisfaction from what they are doing. Can we expect them to give off their best performance? Because of lack of personal satisfaction many organisations have to make do with mediocrity.

- **Workplace environment**. At the workplace, one comes across a variety of people where men and women work together. Is the environment congenial and friendly? Can one work freely without thought of personal security? Are colleagues cooperative? One needs to feel secure and comfortable to be able to focus on giving one's best performance.
- **Working hours**. Generally, one needs to work for eight hours a day. Are the working hours convenient? In many fields, there are two or three shifts with work going on non-stop around the clock. Many fail to adjust to waking up at night and sleeping in the day. Some fall an easy prey to the stress. Are the workers required to do over-time often? Is conveyance made available to reach home late at night? The answers to these questions will provide the necessary information if it is an ideal job.
- **Work experience gained**. An important aspect of every job is the work experience one gains at the workplace. What one learns there is not taught in any college or university. It has to be experienced first hand on the job. Is the work experience useful? Does it add to one's skills and abilities? Will it be useful in the long-term career goals? The answers to these questions can be useful in appreciating the intangible benefits of the job.
- **Opportunities for growth**. Some jobs offer opportunities for growth, while others do not. To safeguard against attrition, which is a major problem in many organisations, many employers ensure that there is a gradual growth to keep the employees attracted.

- **Monetary gains**. Besides other considerations, monetary gains from the job are an important consideration because the money is a source of livelihood for the employee. Is the remuneration consistent with industry standards? Does the job provide opportunities for increments on the basis of time and experience? Everyone desires increasing returns as one grows up in a job. If the job provides this, it would lead to an ideal situation.

- **Social needs**. Every job provides an opportunity to meet new people and make friends. Some of these contacts can lead one to higher positions also. The benefits may not be immediately visible, but they will be beneficial in attaining long-term goals. One should not overlook this aspect of the job.

- **Personal satisfaction**. It is human nature to desire appreciation for doing good work. Does the employer appreciate good work? Or does he take good and mediocre work in the same stride? This may appear to be of little consequence initially, but if good work is not appreciated, one begins to lose interest and employee motivation levels fall.

- **Life balance**. Every employee desires that there should be a fair balance between the home, the workplace and the society. Some time must also be available for personal needs. Does the job provide an opportunity for a reasonable balance between these activities? If it does not, it is likely that life balance would get disturbed, causing frustration.

With all of the above questions answered, you will appreciate whether you could classify the job as ideal. In real life, it is difficult to find ideal situations because of multiple interactions amongst people and situations, each person contributing towards change. A situation would be ideal when a person has the skills and ability to adjust to a variety of circumstances. One does not find an ideal situation. One creates it through an accommodating perception.

Think it over...

The man who does not work for the love of work but only for money is likely to neither make money nor find much fun in life.

— *Charles M. Schwab*

Enjoying Work

For a job to be termed a 'super job', it is necessary that one should enjoy doing it. People often wonder when a person says that he or she enjoys the job. How can a person enjoy a job? What's the fun part in a job? People look at their jobs differently. Some enjoy doing it, while others think it is the daily grind. For a few who rise to great heights, it can also be an obsession. Generally, people who enjoy doing their work rise quickly in their careers. Here are a few ideas in making the work more enjoyable:

- **Work with a positive attitude**. Work is a necessity. If one looks at it with a positive attitude, it becomes easy and satisfying. Always remind yourself that with work completed each day you are moving towards your goals. You are moving towards a better tomorrow.

- **Accept assignments as a challenge**. New assignments need to be completed at the workplace regularly. Accept each assignment as a challenge.

Resolve to give the best of your performance every day. Each challenge will motivate you and prepare you for greater achievements.

- **Celebrate success with others**. Each success adds on to one's confidence. Celebrate your success when you complete your assignment. Go to a movie. Spare some time to meet friends. Find time to watch your favourite programme on TV. Buy yourself a little gift. These little rewards linked with success add pleasure to work.
- **Develop friendships at the workplace**. One comes across a variety of people at the workplace. Some of them may be working with you, while others may be visiting the workplace as customers, clients and suppliers. Building friendships can help you network, which can be a source of future growth.
- **Learn as you work**. Besides the experience people gain at a job, there are several opportunities to learn new skills and techniques which can be very useful. Learning new things at the workplace is always an enjoyable experience.
- **Learn time management**. One of the finest ways of increasing productivity, attaining success and enhancing one's confidence is to learn and practise good time management. The best way is to prioritize your work on a weekly and daily basis. With better utilisation of your time, you will have more time for yourself and leisure.
- **Fun at the workplace**. As children, we were taught that all work and no play make Jack a dull boy. You may not be able to do it right away after joining a job, but in many offices the workers celebrate colleagues'

birthdays and anniversaries at the time of closing office or during coffee/tea break. In some organisations, workers go for picnics and outings once or twice a year.

A Balanced Life

There are four distinct aspects of everyday life that need a person's attention. The first is to fulfill the needs of the family. One needs to provide for their upkeep and upbringing. They require a certain amount of time each day. As a source of livelihood, one needs work or a job. The second is to put in a complete day's work to earn a remuneration that is a source of livelihood to the family. Without this one cannot sustain a family. The third is to have some time for a social life beyond the family. One needs friends and the services of many others who make life worthwhile. The fourth aspect, which is probably the most ignored, is a little time for personal introspection. As long as there is a balance between the four aspects of life, one is at peace and there is a sense of harmony everywhere.

Few people are able to maintain this balance in life. The majority ignores their personal needs and leaves it for a later time of life when they would have more time. In other spheres, work takes most of the time at the cost of the other two. One often comes across workaholics. They are obsessed with work and have very little time for the family or social networking. Those who give too much of their time to the family at the cost of work are left behind at the workplace. Their professional growth is stifled. Those who lay greater emphasis to social networking may grow as leaders but their family and work suffer. It is, therefore, necessary that one must have a fair balance between different aspects of life. Since every individual is unique and looks at the situation from his or her point of view, it is difficult to suggest how time must be divided for each activity. One has to leave it to an individual's choice.

A Good Boss

It would be wrong to term a job as a 'super job' unless one has a good boss. Every worker seeks a good boss, but like most relationships, one does not have a choice in selecting a boss. One has to be satisfied with whatever one gets. At the workplace, bosses come in all shapes and sizes. Most are demanding but not difficult to work with. However, there are a few who are rough and foul-mouthed. It is not that they do not have their strengths. Without them, they would not have been at the workplace. Their perceptions about work relationships may be distorted, or they may lack skills in dealing with people. The important thing is that a boss is a boss and instructions must be obeyed.

With men and women working in every office, one comes across a lot of female bosses. Surveys have indicated that a majority prefer male bosses because they are more focused, take quick decisions and complete assignments faster. One reason for this could be that women are more emotional and part of their attention may be divided towards the home. We cannot overlook that despite all the progress some people are still prejudiced about being led by a lady boss.

Whoever be the boss, he or she becomes good when a person is able to maintain a professional relationship and also deliver what is expected of the job. The problem does not emerge from others. It comes from our own attitude towards people and work. The problems arise from our own thought processes. The moment one adopts an open attitude of acceptance of people and situations every boss becomes a good boss. Accept the boss as a mentor and guide. Do not mix workplace and personal relationships. Accept whatever pertains to the job and choose what else appeals to you. With a person maintaining professional relationships, every boss is fit enough to make your job a 'super job'.

Think it over...

All men, if they work not as in the great taskmaster's eye, will work wrong, work unhappily for themselves and you.

— *Carlyle*

Work Appraisal

It is customary for employers to periodically appraise the work of every employee. Some do it just as a formality, but many do it to assess workers' capabilities, to evaluate both strengths and weaknesses, and use the information for promotions or special assignments where particular skills are required.

A good performance appraisal would always have employee input. The manager and the employee would fill in the appraisals independently and then together confer on the issue. Appraisals should be linked with the organisation goals and what needs to be done. Employees need mentoring and support to give off their best performance. Effective communication plays an important part. Employees should be able to inform how their work has benefited the organisation. Small things add up to much, and unless reminded, many managers overlook useful employee inputs.

Some business consultants insist that appraisals must be done frequently – three to four times a year, and the manager and the employees must discuss issues together to sort out problems when they are still small. When allowed to become big, the problems could cost much in terms of productivity and profitability. Besides, these appraisals help involve and build the employees. These appraisals help employees identify their strengths and weaknesses on the job, and also how they can get over the shortcomings through better work skills.

Enhancing Work Skills

Management gurus repeatedly remind us that a person will attain the height consistent with his or her abilities and no more. From this it is obvious that as long as a person has more work skills than those required for the job he or she is doing, the person is fit to be promoted to the next higher position. This can also be taken to mean that those who desire to keep rising in the workplace must enhance their work skills. This requires upgradation of knowledge pertaining to oneself and the work being done. It is felt one must read the journals and books pertaining to the field of work and also those pertaining to personality development and acquiring new skills. As long as a person possesses more skills than those required for a job, one will find the work easy and can refer to it as a 'super job'. Many ask what special skills need to be continuously enhanced besides the knowledge pertaining to one's field of work. The general consensus is that the following skills require continuous attention:

- **Communication skills**. No amount of emphasis is enough to highlight the importance of good communication skills. One should be able to write and speak well. One must always be conscious whether the communication is effective. Always remember the 5 Cs. The communication must be: **Clear** – It must clearly tell what is to be done; **Concise** – If it is lengthy, the meaning may be misinterpreted; **Courteous** – Requests receive early attention; **Convincing** – Unless the reader is convinced, the communication will not produce results; and **Complete** – There should be no element of doubt in the communication.

- **Speaking skills**. Very few people possess good speaking skills. Even in the top management, only a few are able to speak convincingly to a group of people. That makes this skill very important at the workplace. The best of presentations fall flat when they are not backed by good public speaking skills. One must remember that one is not born a good speaker. Speaking skills have to be learnt like any other skill. To speak well, one must prepare in advance, be focused on the subject, create a rapport with the audience and must speak as much as is necessary and no more.

- **Effective meetings**. Everyone needs to attend a meeting. Most of them are a waste of time. A common cause for their failure is poor communication and handling of the meeting. To succeed, circulate the agenda in advance, be well prepared, begin and end on time, discuss one item at a time, and keep the discussions within control. Do not get provoked in the event of difference of opinion. The meeting must have a definite purpose and each step should carry it towards its goal. Circulate the minutes after the meeting.

- **Work as a team**. Nobody can be as effective as a team pursuing a cause. Most organisations now operate as a big team with smaller teams within it. Teams achieve much more than what can be achieved by individuals working independently. To succeed within a team, one must have a common goal broken down to individual goals. Set definite deadlines. Learn to live in harmony to attain the common goal. Let each team member develop leadership skills.

- **Good relationships**. People say business is people. If you can get along well with people, you can do business. This is true in every sphere of life. It appears an easy thing to do, but one must remember that people are complex human beings and understanding them is a lifetime exercise. One needs to learn every day how to get along well with people. To win over people, make them feel wanted. Listen what they say. Accept whatever is dear to them. Respect their hopes and aspirations.

- **Decision-making**. Decision-making is not as difficult as people imagine it to be. One learns it through experience. Like the ability to get along well with people, the ability to take decisions is amongst the most important skills in human beings. People reach top positions because of their decision-making skills. To learn decision-making, define the problem specifically, collect as many facts as possible, giving due importance to an element of bias, consider the pros and cons from every angle and take an appropriate decision. Do not let anyone force you to a decision.

- ❖ **Time management skills**. It has repeatedly been said that one must utilise one's time to promote productivity. This is one skill which one learns every day. At no stage can one say that I have learnt all that there was to learn. The secret lies in working to priorities. The real skill lies in knowing what is more important than the other. Experience and perseverance are the best teachers.

Think it over...

Man should be ever better than he seem; and shape his acts, and discipline his mind; to walk adorning earth, with hope of heaven.

— *Aubrey de Vere*

A Life Plan

Once again we come back to the life plan every person must have to move upwards. With goals and a plan, one can measure one's progress. As long as the progress is satisfactory, one can say that one is pursuing a 'super job'.

The goals and the plans must be reviewed periodically, and plans should be adjusted whenever it is necessary.

In any job situation, one needs to serve to fulfill the responsibilities attached to the job. While skills and abilities are important, one aspect that needs special attention is that responsibilities must be fulfilled honestly. Honesty and integrity are the hallmarks of all great men and women. People can earn large sums of money and also amass wealth dubiously, but no one is known to enjoy it for long. Time always catches up. Honesty and integrity are qualities of a good character that builds up gradually over the years, accepting virtues and high values as a part of everyday life. The seeds are sown in childhood by caring parents but nurtured through personal effort. A path of honesty is not always easy, but it is the only correct path if one wants to succeed and serve through a 'super job'.

The Résumé

Most people prepare a curriculum vitae or résumé once, and after getting a job forget about it until they are moving into a new job. The résumé is a living document. It must be revised periodically. Even if one does not amend the formal document every time, the additions in terms of new skills acquired, the new experiences gained or new achievements made must be listed for future use. For example, educationists and research professionals continue to list the new papers they present at seminars or the results they have arrived at through new trials and experiments. In the same way, people in every field should continue to amend the résumé for future use. Doctors attend seminars, those in business attend training sessions and even teachers attend seminars on a variety of subjects. With each new experience, the résumé gets richer and one can look forward to harvest the benefits of the time and effort spent on different activities. The résumé eventually becomes a living proof of the journey an individual passes from the beginning of the career till date. It holds special significance for those changing jobs in mid-career period.

Motivation

Serving through a 'super job' requires one to be motivated always. Like a leader, one needs to be a self-starter. One should be ready to take initiative. Success is a great motivator, but before one can attain success, one still needs to be motivated. Different things are known to motivate people. Everyone responds to appreciation and praise. Relaxation, a walk in a garden or park, or a picnic is always motivating. People go to vacations to de-stress and get motivated for more action. People take up hobbies because they are creative and relaxing. Most people respond to different kinds of music. Every individual gradually begins to understand one's own likes and dislikes and finds out what motivates him or her best.

Appreciation and praise are known to have motivated men and women since time immemorial. However, an individual does not control these. One can only perform well. The rest depends upon others. People who need to get ahead must learn to keep themselves motivated. An ideal way is through auto-suggestion. Thoughts of success are always motivating.

Controlling Stress

We discussed stress earlier, and we are at it once again because it is very important in everyday work routine. With competition in every field and with one trying to outdo the other, stress builds up very fast. With specialised training, more young people are occupying important positions in the corporate world. Success is coming earlier in life but not without its toll. Unknown earlier, young people are suffering from burnout or acute stress. Many are seeking support from doctors and psychiatrists. Ask yourself these simple questions to find out if stress is affecting you:

- Do you feel you are more irritable than normal? You are if your colleagues and others ask you if you are feeling all right.
- Do you feel tired most of the time? Rest gives some relief, but the moment you are asked to do something you feel tired.
- Do you keep putting off work to the next day? If you do on the pretext that you are too busy and were attending to unexpected visitors, stress is surely chasing you.
- Do you feel that work is no longer enjoyable and satisfying? You prefer to fritter away the time on activities other than work.
- Do you keep saying you need a break? And when you go on a break, you return from a vacation still feeling tired.

- Do you keep feeling that you need a better quality of sleep? When you wake up, you do not feel sufficiently rested.

If the answers to the above questions are "yes", in all likelihood you need to consult a doctor. However, more than the medicines the doctor may prescribe you, you need to change your thought processes or attitude. When people fail to change their attitude and the medicines are not sufficiently helpful, the doctor guides one to the psychiatrist. This is happening too often every day. When people do not pay heed to signals emerging from the body and continue to overburden the system, one pays a heavy price for it.

Fatigue is partly physical and partly emotional. Physical fatigue builds up because of contracting and relaxing of muscles during work. When the muscles remain contracted for a long period during work, tension builds up in the nerves adjoining the muscles. This tension along with the wear and tear of the muscles causes fatigue. To overcome this fatigue, people drink tea, coffee and alcoholic beverages, and some rely upon massage or drugs. However, the best remedy for physical fatigue is rest. A good night's sleep prepares one for another day. To avoid physical fatigue, it is best to alternate different kinds of work, use comfortable furniture and exercise gently to relax the affected muscles.

To avoid emotional fatigue, one needs to develop a positive attitude towards work. We rely upon work as a source of livelihood, give our best to it, but the moment we begin to get attached to it, feelings and emotions begin to interfere with one's attitude and fatigue begins to build up. One needs to adopt an attitude of trusteeship towards a job.

We are liable to fulfill certain responsibilities towards it and no more. When we become sensitive to every situation and issue at work, the feelings can play havoc and emotional stress takes hold of us. Yoga and meditation are known to keep it in control.

A 'super job' must be free of stress. The job and the employer may appear to be the cause of this stress, but it is not so. In reality, an individual is personally responsible for it and no one else. As long as a person maintains a positive attitude towards work, one will be free of stress.

Think it over...

He who is not contented with what he has would not be contented with what he would like to have.

— *Socrates*

Career Satisfaction

Career satisfaction is important for a job to be termed a 'super job'. Different people derive satisfaction from a variety of things. Money is an important factor to many people. They are happy as long as long as money flows from the job. To a lot of people the satisfaction one derives from something done sincerely and well is very important. The sincerity of purpose gives great inner happiness through a sense of achievement. The satisfaction one derives through careers like teaching where one helps young people build lives, or in medicine when a person saves lives is immeasurable. Every job has its own characteristics and fulfills needs that can be a source of great satisfaction. Look for the satisfaction that emerges from within you by fulfilling a useful need. Career satisfaction helps keep stress away and truly makes it a 'super job'.

Growth Opportunities

Every employer knows that if he wants his employees to work faithfully for him, there must be an element of growth in every job. With time and experience, one must be able to move upwards. To provide this growth, employers incorporate an element of annual increments in the salary, or a bonus given at the end of year. However, the growth employees desire is that which comes from rising to the next higher position. As a measure to convince employees of their growth, many employers give fancy titles like 'assistant manager', 'deputy manager', 'senior manager', 'group manager' and the like at all levels of work. The real growth does not come from fancy titles or positions, but from the quantum of responsibility assigned to an employee. Growth comes from handling more responsibility. This growth is linked directly with a person's skills and would be there to stay. When the job provides opportunities for this growth, it becomes a 'super job'. When a person's enhanced skills are not recognised by an employer, it is natural for a person to look for new pastures.

Changing Jobs

It is very rare that a person takes on a job and continues with it forever. The first job provides an opportunity for experience at the workplace. This experience helps a person to evaluate one's own feelings and career goals and also provides the person an opportunity to study the potential in the field of his or her choice. With better information, a person can take mature decisions pertaining to one's job and career.

Just as employees search for greener pastures to move on to, employers are equally eager to look for people with special skills. First jobs are often a good stepping stone for this purpose. We have earlier discussed what one needs to look for when changing jobs. An important thing is to never close the door behind you. Let the employer know that you are grateful for your association with him, and that you have gained valuable experience that you shall always remember. You never know that he may later invite you to a 'super job' to fill an important position in his organisation.

Points to Ponder...

- The employer and the employee together create a 'super job'.
- Several factors contribute to make a job 'ideal'.
- When a person enjoys working, it becomes a 'super job'.
- There must be a fair balance in the time one spends with the family, at the workplace and in the society.
- It is good relationships that make a boss 'great'.
- Work appraisal is a useful tool for personal growth.
- Continuous upgrading of skills is necessary to rise in a job.

- Honesty and integrity play an important role for a successful life plan.
- The résumé is a living document; upgrade it regularly.
- A motivated person never looks behind.
- Controlling stress is as important as upgrading personal skills.
- A 'super job' must provide satisfaction and growth opportunities.